D0539668

BEST OF
Venice

Damien Simonis

Best of Venice
2nd edition – January 2005
First published – June 2002

Published by Lonely Planet Publications Pty Ltd
ABN 36 005 607 983

Australia	Head Office, Locked Bag 1, Footscray, Vic 3011
	☎ 03 8379 8000 fax 03 8379 8111
	🖳 talk2us@lonelyplanet.com.au
USA	150 Linden St, Oakland, CA 94607
	☎ 510 893 8555 toll free 800 275 8555
	fax 510 893 8572
	🖳 info@lonelyplanet.com
UK	72–82 Rosebery Avenue, London EC1R 4RW
	☎ 020 7841 9000 fax 020 7841 9001
	🖳 go@lonelyplanet.co.uk

This title was commissioned in Lonely Planet's London office and produced by: **Commissioning Editor** Michala Green **Coordinating Editor** Lucy Monie **Managing Editor** Melanie Dankel **Proofer** Laura Gibb **Layout Designer** David Kemp **Cartographers** Kusnandar, Jolyon Philcox, Adrian Persoglia, Tony Fankhauser, Sarah Sloane **Managing Cartographer** Mark Griffiths **Cover Designer** Pepi Bluck **Cover Artwork** Maria Vallianos **Project Managers** Andrew Weatherill, Rachel Imeson **Mapping Development** Paul Piaia **Regional Publishing Manager** Amanda Canning **Thanks to** Kate McDonald, Darren O'Connell, Fiona Siseman, Quentin Frayne, Adriana Mammarella

Photographs by Lonely Planet Images and Juliet Coombe except for the following: p8, p10, p12, p13, p14, p20, p21, p23, p26, p32, p37, p47, p48, p53, p54, p55, p57, p63, p65, p67, p70, p72, p74, p76, p79, p80, p81 Damien Simonis; p9 Roberto Soncin Gerometta; p10 Dallas Stribley; p11 Jon Davison; p15 Gareth McCormack; p21 Jenny Jones. **Cover photograph** A gondola makes its way up the Grand Canal in Venice, Bethune Carmichael/Lonely Planet Images. All images are copyright of the photographers unless otherwise indicated. Many of the images in this guide are available for licensing from Lonely Planet Images: 🖳 www.lonelyplanetimages.com.

ISBN 1 74059 476 2

Printed through The Bookmaker International Ltd. Printed in China

Acknowledgements ACTV Network Map, © 2004

HOW TO USE THIS BOOK

Colour-Coding & Maps

Each chapter has a colour code along the banner at the top of the page which is also used for text and symbols on maps (eg, all venues reviewed in the Highlights chapter are orange on the maps). The fold-out maps inside the front and back covers are numbered from 1 to 5. All sights and venues in the text have map references; eg, (3, J4) means Map 3, grid reference J4. See p96 for map symbols.

Prices

Multiple prices listed with reviews (eg €10/5) usually indicate adult/concession admission to a venue. Concession prices can include child, senior, student, member or coupon discounts. Meal cost and room rate categories are listed at the start of the Eating and Sleeping chapters, respectively.

Text Symbols

☎	telephone
✉	address
🖳	email/website address
€	admission
☾	opening hours
ⓘ	information
⚓	vaporetto/traghetto stop
🚌	bus
P	parking available
♿	wheelchair access
✗	on site/nearby eatery
⚘	child-friendly venue
V	good vegetarian selection

Contents

AUTHOR

Damien Simonis

Damien is hooked: a first, brief encounter with this lady on the lagoon as a fresh-faced backpacker from the Antipodes left an indelible mark. He had to come back, it was just a question of when. Years later he did, but things had changed – Italian had become Damien's second language and he had criss-crossed the bootlike Italian peninsula, on assignment and off. An adolescent infatuation had become something less ingenuous, but the cracks that began to appear beneath the make-up only endeared the place to him more. As Damien learns to tread an ever finer path through the labyrinth of lanes (it's always fun to discover another shortcut!) and potter about in boats on the lagoon, our man in Venice can only confess to being hopelessly enamoured.

Heartfelt thanks to Irina Freguia and Vladi Salvan, who again fell over themselves in their efforts to make me feel at home. Caterina de Cesero & Francesco Lobina get a big *abbraccio* for including me in their Redentore party and generally hanging out. I owe a debt to other friends and acquaintances new and old, including: Federica Rocco, Alberto Toso Fei, Federica Centulani & Bernhard Klein, Antonella Dondi dall'Orologio, Lucialda Lombardi, Sebastiano Giorgi, Etta Lisa Basaldella. *Mille grazie a tutti* for their time, help and companionship. Long may the flag of San Marco wave!

PHOTOGRAPHER

Juliet Coombe

Of the 120 cities Juliet has visited, Venice is still her true love, because of its ethereal charm and theatrical setting. It may be one of the world's most photographed, filmed and written-about places, but however many times she goes there, whether for the Carnevale in February or the Venice International Film Festival in August, she always finds something new and inspiring to rekindle her passion for la Serenissima.

SEND US YOUR FEEDBACK

We love to hear from travellers – your comments keep us on our toes and help make our books better. Our well-travelled team reads every word on what you loved or loathed about this book. Although we cannot reply individually to postal submissions, we always guarantee that your feedback goes straight to the appropriate authors, in time for the next edition – and the most useful submissions are rewarded with a free book. To send us your updates – and find out about LP events, newsletters and travel news – visit our award-winning website: 💻 **www.lonelyplanet.com**.

Note: We may edit, reproduce and incorporate your comments in Lonely Planet products such as guidebooks, websites and digital products, so let us know if you don't want your comments reproduced or your name acknowledged. For a copy of our privacy policy visit 💻 www.lonelyplanet.com/privacy.

Introducing Venice

Decaying, awash in winter and drained of its people, the unique city-on-the-water appears moribund. Yet Venice, like the old courtesan it is frequently compared with, remains unperturbed. She has lost none of her power to bewitch; of all the great Italian cities, Venice remains the most beguiling.

The lagoon city, which rose to become Europe's most powerful merchant empire and was known as la Serenissima, the Most Serene, captivates merely by its appearance. One of the simplest and most inexhaustible joys is to wander the narrow canalside lanes, cross the innumerable bridges and get lost in the labyrinth. In no other city can it be said that the main form of transport is your own feet…followed by boat! Listen – no cars. Some choose to live here for that reason alone.

Venice is a festival of culture, a High Renaissance banquet. Tiepolo, Tintoretto and Titian are at the head of a roll call too long to contemplate. The very city is a magnificent work of art, an extraordinary catalogue ranging from Romanesque and Veneto–Byzantine to Gothic and the rational magnificence of Palladio. It is a crucible of creeds, a meeting point of East and West.

Tourists flock to it like the pigeons of San Marco, tacky restaurants and souvenir stands abound and the gondola ride has become a cheesy obligation. But you need little imagination, just the curiosity to get off the main trails, to plunge into the romance and melancholy of it all, cradled by the lapping of the lagoon's waters.

La Serenissima after a storm at dusk, San Marco (pp8–9)

Seen from the air, Venice looks like a juicy slab of sole served up on a glittering platter, crossed with a dash of sauce in the shape of a reverse 's'. This is the *centro storico* (Venice proper), the core of the modern municipality of Venice, which covers the surrounding lagoon and islands (p34) as well as strips of the adjacent mainland.

The city has been divided into six quarters *(sestieri)* since the 12th century. Clockwise from the train station they are: Cannaregio, Castello, San Marco, Dorsoduro, San Polo and Santa Croce.

After the Grand Canal itself, the world's most romantic Main Street, one's thoughts turn immediately to the central square, Piazza San Marco (p32), dominated by the sumptuous Basilica di San Marco (pp8–9) and Gothic Palazzo Ducale (p10), long the religious and political headquarters of the city. The *sestiere* around it, **San Marco**, is the heart of Venice chic and swarms with activity as visitors and locals converge on it for business, pleasure and shopping.

To the east sprawls **Castello**, once the furnace of Venetian industrial prowess centred on the Arsenale (p26), where la Serenissima's conquering fleets were built. It is a curious mix of workaday 'suburb' and, at its edge, residential tranquillity, full of agreeable surprises and home to the Biennale (p32).

Off the Beaten Track

Chug across to Giudecca, where Palladio's Chiesa del SS Redentore (p31) can be used as a cultural 'excuse' to wander around this intriguing residential island. For some shade, stroll in the Giardini Pubblici (p36) in Castello and the little-visited Isola di San Pietro (p28).

To really get away from it all, take a ferry to le Vignole (p34) or Sant'Erasmo (p35). Once the garden farm islands of Venice, they are havens of tranquillity.

Get some peace in Giudecca

Some of the city's greatest art treasures are held in collections in **Dorsoduro**, south over the Ponte dell'Accademia, and the presence of the university gives it a fresh, young hum, particularly in the bars around Campo Santa Margherita. Separated from it by the Canale della Giudecca waterway lies the peaceful island haven of Giudecca (p34).

San Polo is gathered in around the Rialto markets (p49), which has long been the centre of business, banking and trade empire gossip. Its narrow lanes are crammed with boutiques and fascinating traditional eateries. Quieter is the adjacent area of **Santa Croce**, whose western extremities have a grittier, portside feel. Two bridges link it with **Cannaregio**, a feast of variety from the Jewish Ghetto (p17) to the student revelry of the bars and restaurants around Fondamenta della Misericordia.

Itineraries

Millions of visitors pour into Venice yearly for visits of just two or three days. They run from first-timers to lagoon-oholics in search of hitherto undiscovered nooks and crannies. A wanderer's city, there is no shortage of novelty around just about every corner.

Venice is a chocolate box of fine art and architecture. From Palladio's sleek-lined churches (witness the Chiesa di San Giorgio Maggiore) to the delightful Chiesa di Santa Maria dei Miracoli; from Tintoretto's masterpieces in the Scuola Grande di San Rocco to Titians in the Gallerie dell'Accademia, the list is endless.

A **Museum Pass** (adult/student €15.50/10; valid 3 months) covers entry to a selection of the city's grand sights, including the Palazzo Ducale, Ca' Rezzonico and Ca' Pesaro. There are several variations on this pass.

The orange version of the **Venice Card** (☎ 041 24 24; www.venicecard.it) includes access to an array of sights. See p83.

DAY ONE

Catch the No 1 *vaporetto* to Piazza San Marco (p32) and visit the Basilica di San Marco (pp8–9). Follow with a coffee at Caffè Florian (p60). Cross Ponte dell'Accademia (p33) for some serious art at the Gallerie dell'Accademia (p12) and Peggy Guggenheim Collection (p13).

DAY TWO

Sniff around the Rialto markets (p49) and shops in San Polo (p43). Follow with high culture at the Frari (p14) and the Scuola Grande di San Rocco (p15). After losing the afternoon meandering in Dorsoduro (p44), eat and drink the night away on and around Campo Santa Margherita (p32).

DAY THREE

Explore the Palazzo Ducale (p10), climb the Campanile (p32) and take the ferry to Murano (pp34–5) and Burano (p18). Back in Venice, take a gondola ride (p36), then have a classy meal and a Bellini at Harry's Bar (p64).

Putting the Campanile (p32) in a puddle

BASILICA DI SAN MARCO (3, J4)

Ah, the glory of Venice. For centuries admirers have flocked to admire the dazzling mantle of St Mark's Basilica, a cornucopia of gold and jewels, of untold artistic wealth. The story of the basilica is also one of theft. From the alleged body of St Mark, whisked away from Egypt, to the grand quadriga of bronze horses taken from Constantinople centuries later, not all is holier than thou in the history of St Mark's. Consecrated in 1094, the church embodies a magnificent blend of styles, ranging from Byzantine and Romanesque to Gothic and Renaissance. Built on a Greek cross plan, with five bulbous domes, it became Venice's cathedral in 1807. The only original entrance to the church is the one on the south side that leads to the *battistero* (baptistery). It is fronted by two pillars plundered and brought to Venice from Acre in the Holy Land in the 13th century. The Syriac sculpture, *Tetrarchi* (Tetrarchs), next to the Porta della Carta of the Palazzo Ducale, dates from the 4th century and is believed to represent Diocletian and his three co-emperors, who ruled the Roman Empire in the 3rd century AD.

The arches above the main entrance boast fine mosaics. The one at the left-hand end, depicting the arrival of St Mark's smuggled body in Venice, was completed in 1270. Above the doorway next to it is an 18th-century mosaic depicting the *doge* (duke) venerating St Mark's body.

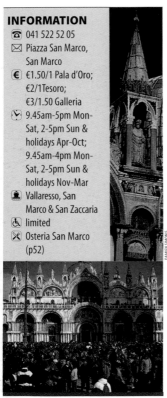

INFORMATION
- ☎ 041 522 52 05
- ✉ Piazza San Marco, San Marco
- € €1.50/1 Pala d'Oro; €2/1Tesoro; €3/1.50 Galleria
- ◷ 9.45am-5pm Mon-Sat, 2-5pm Sun & holidays Apr-Oct; 9.45am-4pm Mon-Sat, 2-5pm Sun & holidays Nov-Mar
- ⬤ Vallaresso, San Marco & San Zaccaria
- ♿ limited
- ✗ Osteria San Marco (p52)

DAMIEN SIMONIS

The impressive entrance of San Marco

On the **Loggia dei Cavalli** above the main entrance are copies of four gilded bronze horses; the originals, on display inside, were stolen by the Venetian expeditionary force when Constantinople was sacked in 1204, during the Fourth Crusade.

Through the doors is the **narthex**, or vestibule, its domes and arches decorated with mosaics, mainly dating from the 13th century. The oldest mosaics in the basilica, dating from 1063, are in the niches of the bay in front of the main door from the narthex into the church. They feature the Madonna with the apostles.

The **interior** of the basilica is dazzling. The exquisite 12th-century marble pavement, an infinite variety of geometrical whimsy interspersed with floral and animal motifs, is complemented by a feast of gilded **mosaics** on the walls and ceilings. Work started on them in the 11th century and continued for hundreds of years. Notable mosaics include: the 12th-century Ascension in the central dome; the early 12th–century mosaics of the Pentecost in the west dome; the 13th-century lunette over the west door depicting Christ between the Virgin and St Mark.

> **Dress Code**
> A strict dress code operates at the basilica. You will not be allowed in with shorts on (unless they cover the knees) and women must cover their shoulders and upper arms. People are turned away every day, often after queuing for hours, for not respecting this rule.

A magnificent, multicoloured marble **iconostasis** (another Byzantine element) separates the main body of the church from the area before the altar. Dividing the iconostasis in two is a huge cross of bronze and silver; to each side, the Virgin Mary and the Apostles line up. In a crypt beneath the majestic marble *altar maggiore* (high altar) lie the remains of St Mark.

Behind the altar is the exquisite **Pala d'Oro**, a gold-, enamel- and jewel-encrusted altarpiece made in Constantinople for Doge Pietro Orseolo I in 976, which has been added to over the centuries. Almost 2000 precious stones adorn it.

The **Tesoro** (Treasury), accessible from the right transept, contains most of the booty from the 1204 raid on Constantinople, including a thorn said to be from the crown worn by Christ.

Through a door at the far right end of the narthex, stairs lead to the **Galleria** (aka Museo di San Marco), which contains the original gilded bronze horses (see opposite) and the Loggia dei Cavalli. The Galleria affords wonderful views of the church's interior, while the loggia offers equally splendid vistas of the square.

DON'T MISS
- 13th-century Romanesque carvings on three arches of the main doorway
- Mosaics when the basilica is illuminated: from 11.30am to 12.30pm and during mass at weekends
- Mosaics between the windows of the apse depicting St Mark and three other patron saints of Venice, among the earliest mosaics in the basilica

ROBERTO SONCIN GEROMETTA

PALAZZO DUCALE   (3, J5)

The Doge's Palace is a rare example of civil Venetian Gothic and was home to the *doge* and to all arms of government, including prisons, for much of the thousand or so years of the Republic.

Established in the 9th century, the building began to assume its present form 500 years later. The palace's two magnificent Gothic façades in white Istrian stone and pink Veronese marble face Piazzetta San Marco.

From the main courtyard you ascend several stairways to reach the rooms comprising the Appartamento del Doge (Duke's Apartments). Among these, the grand **Sala delle Mappe** contains maps dating from 1762 that depict the Republic's territories and the voyages of Marco Polo.

Upstairs are the rooms where the highest sectors of government met. Among these, the **Anticollegio** features four Tintorettos and the *Ratto d'Europa* (Rape of Europa) by Veronese. Further on is the splendid **Sala del Collegio**, the ceiling of which features works by Veronese and Tintoretto. Signs lead you downstairs to the immense **Sala del Maggiore Consiglio** (Hall of the Grand Council), dominated by Tintoretto's *Paradiso*, one of the world's largest oil paintings.

A trail of corridors leads you to the enclosed **Ponte dei Sospiri** (Bridge of Sighs). The bridge is split into two levels, allowing for traffic heading into and out of the **Prigioni Nuove** (New Prisons); these were built on the east side of the canal to cater for the overflow from the **Prigioni Vecchie** (Old Prisons), which are within the Palace itself.

DON'T MISS

- Museo dell'Opera
- Veronese's paintings in the Sala del Consiglio dei Dieci
- Prigioni Nuove
- Itinerari Secreti (Secret Itineraries, a guided tour of lesser known parts of the palace)

DAMIEN SIMONIS

DALLAS STRIBLEY

GRAND CANAL (3-5)

This is Main St Venice, a broad ribbon of colours, sounds and smells in the shape of an inverted 'S'. Jump on the No 1 all-stops *vaporetto* (water bus) at Piazzale Roma (3, A2) or Ferrovia (3, B1) for the half-hour meander along the world's most extraordinary traffic artery.

INFORMATION
- ✉ Grand Canal
- € €3.50 (return €6)
- 🔊 Stops all along the Grand Canal
- ♿ fair

The 3.5km canal, probably once a natural extension of the River Brenta before the latter was diverted, supports an ever-changing parade of transport barges, *vaporetti*, water taxis, private speedboats, gondolas, police patrol boats, water ambulances and water fire brigade. The floating pageant is backed on either side by more than 100 *palazzi* (mansions) dating from the 12th to the 18th centuries.

Just after the Riva de Biasio stop (4, B3) is the **Fondaco dei Turchi** (p24), recognisable by the three-storey towers on either side of its colonnade.

Past Rio di San Marcuola, the **Palazzo Vendramin-Calergi** (p28) is on the left. To the right, just after the San Stae stop (3, E1), you'll see **Ca' Pesaro** (p16). Shortly after, to the left, is the **Ca' d'Oro** (p20), beyond which the boat turns towards the 16th-century **Ponte di Rialto** (p33) and the **Rialto markets** (p49).

DON'T MISS
- Ca' Foscari (3, D4)
- Palazzo Grassi (3, D4)
- Palazzo Dario's marble façade (3, F6)
- Palazzo Corner (3, F6)

The *vaporetto* sweeps on past more fine mansions to the wooden **Ponte dell'Accademia** (p33), where you get off for the art gallery of the same name (p12), and on past the grand **Chiesa di Santa Maria della Salute** (p22) before reaching San Marco.

The world's most extraordinary traffic artery

JON DAVISON

GALLERIE DELL'ACCADEMIA (3, D6)

The Gallerie dell'Accademia, housed in a former church and convent, boasts a swathe of works that follows the mastery of Venetian art from the 14th to the 18th centuries.

INFORMATION

☎ 041 520 03 45
🖥 www.gallerieaccad emia.org
✉ Campo della Carità, Dorsoduro 1050
€ adult/EU citizens 18-25 yrs old/child under 12 & EU citizens under 18 & over 65 €6.50/3.25/free
🕙 8.15am-2pm Mon, 8.15am-7.15pm Tue-Sun
ℹ audioguide €4
🚊 Accademia
♿ limited
🍴 Ai Gondolieri (p53)

DAMIEN SIMONIS

Room (Sala) 2 contains a number of paintings by Giovanni Bellini, Vittore Carpaccio and Cima da Conegliano. Carpaccio's altarpiece *Crocifissione e Apoteosi dei 10,000 Martiri del Monte Ararat* (Crucifixion and Apotheosis of the 10,000 Martyrs of Mt Ararat) is an extraordinary study in massacre and martyrdom.

In **Rooms 4** and **5** you can enjoy a mixed bag, including Andrea Mantegna's *San Giorgio* (St George) and works by Jacopo Bellini and son Giovanni. Particularly striking are the rare contributions by Giorgione: *La Tempesta* (The Storm) and *La Vecchia* (The Old Woman). The latter is ahead of its time, readily identifiable with 19th-century portraiture.

Major works adorn **Room 10** and Paolo Veronese's *Convito in Casa di Levi* (Feast in the House of Levi) is one of the highlights. Also on display is one of Titian's last works, his disturbing *Pietà*.

Rooms 12 to 19 are of lesser interest but **Room 20** is a revelation. The crowd scenes, splashes of red and activity pouring from the canvases in the cycle dedicated to the *Miracoli della Vera Croce* (Miracles of the True Cross) are a vivid record of Venetian life by Carpaccio, Gentile Bellini and others.

Carpaccio's extraordinary series of nine paintings recounting the life of Santa Orsola, in **Room 21**, is the collection's last high point.

DAMIEN SIMONIS

DON'T MISS

- Tintoretto's *Assunzione della Vergine* and *Trafugamento del Corpo di San Marco*
- Tiepolo's *Castigo dei Serpenti*
- Art in the former Chiesa di Santa Maria della Carità
- Titian's *Presentazione di Maria al Tempio*

PEGGY GUGGENHEIM COLLECTION (3, E6)

The eccentric millionaire art collector Peggy Guggenheim called the unfinished **Palazzo Venier dei Leoni** home for 30 years, until she died in 1979. She left behind, apart from her cherished dogs now buried with her in the sculpture garden, a collection of works by her favourite modern artists, representing most of the major art movements of the 20th century.

Most of the collection is in the **east wing**. Early Cubist paintings include Picasso's *Poet* (1911) and *Pipe, Glass, Bottle of Vieux Marc* (1914), and Georges Braque's *Clarinet* (1912). The list of greats is long and you'll want a couple of hours to complete a tour of the collection. There are a couple of Kandinskys, including his *Upward* (1929). Interesting works from Spain include Dalí's *Birth of Liquid Desires* (1932) and Miró's *Seated Woman II* (1939).

Among the many paintings by Max Ernst, Guggenheim's husband and doyen of Surrealism, is the disturbing *Antipope* (1942). Other names to look for include: Jackson Pollock, Mark Rothko, Willem de Kooning, Paul Delvaux, Alexander Calder, Juan Gris, Kurt Schwitters, Paul Klee, Francis Bacon, Giorgio de Chirico, Piet Mondrian and Marc Chagall. Out in the **sculpture garden** are several curious pieces by Henry Moore and Jean Arp.

INFORMATION

- ☎ 041 240 54 11
- ⌨ www.guggenheim-venice.it
- ✉ Palazzo Venier dei Leoni, Dorsoduro 701
- € adult/senior/student & child €10/8/5
- ☼ 10am-6pm Wed-Mon, 10am-10pm Sat Apr-Oct
- ⓘ museum guides available at entrance & shop
- ⚓ Accademia
- ♿ good
- 🍴 museum café

DAMIEN SIMONIS

Peggy's Peregrinations

Miss Guggenheim came into her fortune in 1921 and set off for Europe where she became interested in contemporary art and opened a gallery (Guggenheim Jeune in London). As the Nazis bore down on Paris in 1940, Peggy was there looking for potential acquisitions. She spent the war in New York and moved to Venice in 1947.

The rear of the mansion hosts a separate collection of Italian Futurists and other modern artists from the peninsula, including Giorgio Morandi, Giacomo Balla and one work by Amedeo Modigliani.

SANTA MARIA GLORIOSA DEI FRARI   (3, D3)

This spare Gothic brick church impresses with its high vaulted ceiling and its sheer size; it was built for the Franciscans in the 14th and 15th centuries on a Latin cross plan (with three naves and a transept). A visit inside is a must on any art lover's tour of the city.

INFORMATION

- ✉ Campo dei Frari, San Polo 3004
- € €2.50 or Chorus ticket
- ☾ 9am-6pm Mon-Sat, 1-6pm Sun
- 🚇 San Tomà
- ♿ limited
- ✕ Osteria San Pantalon (p53)

The simplicity of the interior (red and white marble floor, with the same colours dominating the walls and ceiling) is more than off-set by the extravagance of its decoration in the form of paintings and funereal monuments. The middle of the central nave is filled by voluminous choir stalls, an unusual appearance in an Italian church.

The mastery of **Titian** is, however, decidedly the main attraction of the Frari. His dramatic *Assunta* (Assumption; 1518), which is positioned over the high altar, represents a key moment in his rise as one of the city's greatest artists, praised unreservedly by all and sundry as a work of inspired genius.

Another of his masterpieces, the *Madonna di Ca' Pesaro* (Madonna of Ca' Pesaro), hangs above the Pesaro altar (in the left-hand aisle, near the choir stalls). Also of note are Giovanni Bellini's triptych, in the apse of the sacristy, and Donatello's statue *Giovanni Battista* (John the Baptist), in the first chapel to the right of the high altar.

Chorus Line

An organisation called Chorus offers visitors a special ticket (€8/5) providing entry to 15 outstanding churches. Entrance to individual churches is €2.50. Among the most striking options are: Santa Maria Gloriosa dei Frari, Santa Maria dei Miracoli, San Polo, Sant'Alvise, La Madonna dell'Orto, I Gesuati, San Pietro di Castello, Il Redentore and San Sebastian. The ticket, available from any of the churches, also includes the possibility of visiting the Tesoro (Treasury) in the Basilica di San Marco. See www.chorusvenezia.org for more details.

DAMIEN SIMONIS

SCUOLA GRANDE DI SAN ROCCO (3, C3)

Antonio Scarpagnino's (c1505–49) Renaissance **façade** (exhibiting a hint of the baroque to come), with its white-marble columns and overbearing magnificence, seems uncomfortably squeezed into the tight space of the narrow square below it. Whatever you make of the exterior of this religious confraternity, or *scuola*, dedicated to St Roch, nothing can prepare you for what lies inside.

After winning a competition to decide who would decorate the school (Veronese was among his rivals), **Tintoretto** went on to devote 23 years of his life to this work. The overwhelming concentration of more than 50 paintings by the master is altogether too much for the average human to digest.

Chronologically speaking, you should start upstairs (Scarpagnino designed the staircase) in the **Sala Grande Superiore**. Here you can pick up mirrors to carry around to avoid getting a sore neck while inspecting the ceiling paintings (which depict Old Testament episodes). Around the walls are scenes from the New Testament. A handful of works by other artists (such as Titian, Giorgione and Tiepolo) can also be seen. To give your eyes

INFORMATION

- ☎ 041 523 48 64
- 🖥 www.sanrocco.it
- ✉ Campo San Rocco, Dorsoduro 3052
- € adult/18-26 yr olds/child under 18 €5.50/4/1.50
- 🕒 9am-5.30pm Easter-Oct, 10am-4pm Nov-Easter
- 🚊 San Tomà
- ♿ limited
- 🍴 Osteria San Pantalon (p53)

GARETH McCORMACK

Façade of the Scuola Grande di San Rocco

Plague Prevention

St Roch was born in Montpellier (France) in 1295, and at the age of 20 began wandering through Italy and southern France helping victims of the plague whom he encountered. He died in 1327 and a cult soon grew around his name. His body was transferred to Venice as a kind of plague prevention measure in 1485.

a rest from the paintings, inspect the woodwork below them – it is studded with curious designs, including a false book collection.

Downstairs, the walls of the confraternity's **assembly hall** feature a series on the life of the Virgin Mary, starting on the left wall with the *Annunciazione* and ending with the *Assunzione* opposite.

CA' PESARO (3, F1)

Ca' Pesaro was designed for one of Venice's patrician families by Longhena in a muted baroque style much influenced by the harmonious Renaissance ideas of Sansovino. It was finished in 1710 by Antonio Gaspari after Longhena's death. Since 1902 it has housed the **Galleria d'Arte Moderna** (Modern Art Gallery), which includes works purchased from the Biennale art festival and an eclectic array of Italian and international modern art.

The *androne* (main ground floor hall) is typical of the great patricians' mansions in Venice. You can look out over the Grand Canal from one side, while the inland end gives on to a sunny courtyard with a fountain. The building is as worthy of admiration as the collections it houses.

INFORMATION

- ☎ 041 524 06 95
- 🖳 www.museicivici veneziani.it
- ✉ Fondamenta de Ca' Pesaro, Santa Croce 2076
- € €5.50/3
- 🕓 10am-6pm Tue-Sun Apr-Oct, 10am-5pm Tue-Sun Nov-Mar
- 🚢 San Stae
- ♿ limited
- 🍴 Vecio Fritolin (p55)

"Art is not where you think you're going to find it."
Patrick Mimran

Ca' Pesaro

The art starts with late-19th-century Venetian artists (such as Giacomo Favretto with scenes from Venice) and other Italians. International contributions include Klimt's *Judith II (Salomé)* and artists ranging from Kandinsky and Chagall through Henri Matisse and Paul Klee to Spain's Joaquim Sorolla. Next come striking sculptures by the Milanese Adolfo Widt and then the eclectic De Lisi collection, with works by De Chirico, Miró, Kandinsky and Yves Tanguy, among others. Max Ernst, Henry Moore and others feature in a room dedicated to the 1940s and 1950s.

Upstairs is the intriguing **Museo d'Arte Orientale**, one of the most important collections in Europe of Edo-period art and objects from Japan. It includes armour, weapons, porcelain, artworks and countless household objects.

DON'T MISS

- Auguste Rodin's *Il Pensatore* (The Thinker)
- Kandinsky's *Tre Triangoli* (Three Triangles)
- The classic *terrazzo alla veneziana* floors, typical of Venetian mansions
- The Indonesian shadow puppet collection

GHETTO (4, C1 & B2)

The first records of Jews in Venice (Ashkenazi of German and Eastern European origins) date back to the 10th century. In 1516 all Jews were ordered to live in one area. The Getto Novo (New Foundry) was considered ideal, being surrounded by water – a natural prison. The Ashkenazis' harsh Germanic pronunciation gave us the word 'ghetto'.

Jews could move freely through the city if they wore a yellow cap or badge by day. At midnight gates around the Getto Novo were shut by Christian guards financed by the Jewish community, and reopened at dawn.

INFORMATION
- 🖳 www.ghetto.it
- ✉ Campo di Ghetto Nuovo, Cannaregio 2902/b
- € €8/6.50 for tour of ghetto & Museo Ebraico
- 🚊 Guglie
- ♿ limited
- 🍴 Gam Gam (p56)

The ghetto was tiny and overcrowding turned the buildings around Campo di Ghetto Nuovo into 'skyscrapers' – some apartment blocks have seven storeys, with low ceilings. Atop three were built modest *schole* (synagogues). The **Schola Tedesca** (German Synagogue) is above the building that now houses the **Museo Ebraico** (Jewish Musem; ☎ 041 71 53 59; Campo di Ghetto Nuovo, Cannaregio 2902/b; 🕐 10am-7pm Sun-Fri Jun-Sep, 10am-4.30pm Sun-Fri Oct-May, except Jewish holidays). Virtually next door is the **Schola Canton** (Corner Synagogue) and further around is the **Schola Italiana**, the simplest of the three.

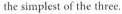

Jews of Venice

From 1541 until 1553, Venice's Jewish community thrived. Its trade was welcome and the community built a reputation for book printing. Then Pope Julian banned such activities and things went downhill. In 1797 Napoleon abolished restrictions on Jews and by 1866 all minorities had been guaranteed equality. In 1943 many of Venice's 1670 Jews were interned and some 200 wound up in a Nazi death camp. Only a handful of Jews live in the Ghetto today.

In 1541 waves of Sephardi Jews from Spain and Portugal arrived, many of them wealthy merchants, and the town authorities ceded another small area to the Jews, the Getto Vecio (Old Foundry), or Ghetto Vecchio. Here the Spanish and Portuguese built their two beautiful synagogues, the **Schola Spagnola** (at the southern end of Campiello della Schole) and the **Schola Levantina**. Guided tours are available (🕐 half-hourly to hourly 10.30am-5.30pm Sun-Fri, except Jewish holidays).

BURANO (5, E1)

Famous for its lace industry, Burano is a pretty fishing village, its streets and canals lined with pastel-coloured houses. The bonbon colours apparently have their origins in the fishermen's desire to see their own houses when heading home from a day at sea – the gay colours are certainly engaging. Given the island's distance from Venice (it takes about 40 minutes to get there), the feeling of having arrived somewhere only fleetingly touched by la Serenissima is inescapable; Burano seems to have an even deeper quietude. **Museo del Merletto** (☎ 041 73 00 34; www.museiciviciveneziani.it; Piazza Galuppi 187; €4/2.50 ☉ 10am-5pm Wed-Mon Apr-Oct, 10am-4pm Wed-Mon Nov-Mar), is Burano's lace-making museum. The islanders became famous for their lace in the late 19th century after the industry was resuscitated and lace-making schools were set up. If you buy lace on the island, choose with care, as much of the cheaper stuff is factory produced. That said, you can still see women stitching away in the shade of their homes and in the parks.

INFORMATION
- 🚉 Burano
- ♿ limited
- 🍴 Al Gatto Nero

If you make the effort to visit (most people take in Murano and Torcello on the same trip), try to give yourself time to wander into the quietest corners and shady parks. Cross the wooden bridge to neighbouring **Mazzorbo** (which has its own *vaporetto* stop), a larger island with a few houses, a couple of trattorias and open green space. A snooze in the grass takes you light years from the monumental overdose of Venice.

A Stitch in Time

Venetian lace was a much sought-after commodity from the 15th century onwards, but was eclipsed by French production in the 18th century. The industry was saved from extinction when lace schools were founded on the island of Burano, largely to alleviate poverty, at the end of the 19th century.

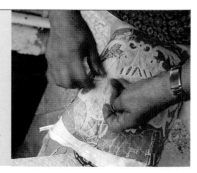

TORCELLO (5, F1)

This delightful island, with its overgrown main square and sparse, scruffy-looking buildings and monuments, was at its peak from the mid-7th century to the 13th century, when it was the seat of the bishop of mainland Altinum (modern Altino) and home to 20,000 souls. Today, fewer than 80 people remain.

Less than a 10-minute walk from the *vaporetto* stop lies the square around which huddles all that remains of old Torcello – the lasting homes of the clergy and the island's secular rulers.

The **Cattedrale di Santa Maria Assunta** was founded in the 7th century and was Venice's first – in the early days this was the leading lagoon settlement. What you see of the church today dates from its first expansion in 824 and rebuilding in 1008. It is therefore about the oldest Venetian monument to have remained relatively untampered with.

The three apses (the central one dates from the original structure) have a Romanesque quality. The magnificent **Byzantine mosaics** inside, dating from the 12th and 13th centuries, are fascinating. On the western wall is a vast mosaic depicting the Last Judgment. Hell (lower right side) does not look any fun at all. The greatest treasure is the mosaic of the Madonna in the half-dome of the central apse. Starkly set on a pure gold background, the figure is one of the most stunning works of Byzantine art you will see in Italy.

It is also possible to climb the **bell tower**, from which you'll be greeted by great views across the island and lagoon.

INFORMATION
- ☎ 041 73 00 84 (cattedrale)
- ✉ Torcello
- € €3 cattedrale; €2 bell tower; or €6 incl Museo di Torcello
- ☽ 10.30am-5.30pm Mar-Oct, 10am-5pm Nov-Feb
- ⓘ audioguides for mosaics in cathedral
- 🚊 Torcello
- ♿ limited
- 🍴 Locanda Cipriani (p71)

Museo di Torcello

DON'T MISS
- Chiesa di Santa Fosca
- Palazzo del Consiglio
- Museo di Torcello

CA' D'ORO (3, F1)

This magnificent 15th-century Gothic structure got its name (Golden House) from the gilding that originally decorated the façade's sculptural details. Visible from the Grand Canal, the façade (even without the shimmering gold) stands out from the rest of the edifice, drab by comparison.

Ca' d'Oro houses the **Galleria Franchetti**, an impressive collection of bronzes, tapestries and paintings. The first floor is devoted mainly to religious painting, sculpture and bronzes from the 15th and early 16th centuries. One of the first items you'll see is a polyptych recounting the martyrdom of San Bartolomeo (St Bartholomew). The violence is remarkable, as is the saintly indifference with which Bartholomew accepts his torment! Much of what you see on this floor is Venetian, but one room has been set aside for Tuscan art.

INFORMATION

- ☎ 041 523 87 90
- ✉ Calle di Ca' d'Oro, Cannaregio 3931
- € €5/2.50
- ⏱ 8.15am-2pm Mon, 8.15am-7.15pm Tue-Sun
- ⛴ Ca' d'Oro
- ♿ limited
- ✕ Osteria dalla Vedova (p57)

On the second floor you can see a series of fragments of frescoes saved from the outside of the Fondaco dei Tedeschi (p27), an important trading house that is now home to the central post office. All but one are by Titian. The other, a nude by Giorgione, is the most striking. Also on this floor is a mixed collection, including works by Tintoretto, Carpaccio, Mantegna, Vivarini, Titian, Signorelli and Van Eyck.

A big incentive for visiting is the chance to lean out over the Grand Canal from the balconies on the 1st and 2nd floors.

The Star & His Master

Titian has been called the 'sun amidst the stars'. But he started under the direction of Giorgione and experts have difficulty distinguishing some of their works. They first collaborated on the Fondaco dei Tedeschi frescoes. Even after Giorgione's death in 1510, Titian continued to work under the spell of his former master.

SAN GIORGIO MAGGIORE (2, F5)

On the island of the same name, Palladio's Chiesa di San Giorgio Maggiore has one of the most prominent positions in Venice and, although it inspired mixed reactions among the architect's contemporaries, it had a significant influence on Renaissance architecture.

Built between 1565 and 1580, it is possibly Palladio's most imposing structure in Venice. The **façade**, although not erected until the following century, is believed to conform with Palladio's wishes. The massive columns on high plinths, crowning tympanum and statues contain an element of sculptural chiaroscuro, casting strong shadows and reinforcing the impression of strength. Facing the Bacino di San Marco and the heart of Venice, its effect is deliberately theatrical.

Inside, the sculptural decoration is sparse, the open space regimented by powerful clusters of columns and covered by luminous vaults.

San Giorgio Maggiore's **art treasures** include Tintoretto's *Ultima Cena* (Last Supper) and the *Raccolta della Manna* (Shower of Manna) on the walls of the high altar, and a *Deposizione* (Deposition) in the Cappella dei Morti. Take the lift to the top of the 60m-high **bell tower** for an extraordinary view.

INFORMATION
- ☎ 041 522 7827
- ✉ San Giorgio Maggiore, Giudecca
- € free, bell tower €3
- ⊙ 9.30am-12.30pm & 2-6pm
- ⛴ San Giorgio
- ♿ limited

San Giorgio Maggiore: sculptural chiaroscuro

An Ignoble Fate

The great Benedictine convent of San Giorgio Maggiore was suppressed after the fall of the Venetian Republic in 1797. The island was turned into a free port and the Austrians set up an artillery base here. By the end of WWII, the island had fallen into decay, only to be saved by the Fondazione Cini.

Behind the church are the grounds of the former monastery. Established in the 10th century by the Benedictines, it was rebuilt in the 13th century and expanded over the 16th century, finishing with the library built by Longhena in the 1640s. Little can be seen, as the **Fondazione Cini**, a cultural foundation, bought it in 1951.

SANTA MARIA DELLA SALUTE (3, G6)

Baldassare Longhena's dazzling white monolith is possibly the city's most familiar silhouette (viewed from Piazzetta San Marco or the Ponte dell'Accademia), but seen from close up it's difficult to take in.

INFORMATION

- ☎ 041 522 55 58
- ✉ Campo della Salute, Dorsoduro 1/b
- € sacristy €1.50
- ☉ 9am-noon & 3-6pm
- 🚊 Salute
- ♿ limited
- ✗ Lineadombra (p53)

A grand salute to the Virgin Mary

Longhena got the commission to build the church, which was to honour the Virgin Mary, who was believed to have delivered the city from an outbreak of plague in 1630. The ranks of statues that festoon the exterior of the church culminate in one of the Virgin Mary atop the dome.

The octagonal form of the church is unusual. Longhena's idea was to design it in the form of a crown for the mother of God. The interior is flooded with light pouring through windows in the walls and dome. Dominating the main body of the church is the baroque **altar maggiore** (high altar), in which is imbedded an icon of Mary brought to Venice from Crete.

The **sacristy** ceiling is bedecked with three remarkable Titians. The figures depicted are so full of curvaceous movement they seem to be caught in a washing machine! The three scenes are replete with high emotion, depicting the struggles between *Caino e Abele* (Cain and Abel), *David e Golia* (David and Goliath) and finally between Abraham and his conscience in *Il Sacrificio di Isaaco* (The Sacrifice of Isaac). The other star of the sacristy is Tintoretto's *Le Nozze di Cana* (The Wedding Feast of Cana), filled with an unusual amount of bright and cheerful light by Tintoretto's rather dark standards.

Walking on Water

Every year, on 21 November, a procession takes place from Piazza San Marco to the Santa Maria della Salute church to give thanks for the city's good health. The last part of the march takes place on a pontoon bridge thrown out between the Santa Maria del Giglio *traghetto* stop and the church.

SS GIOVANNI E PAOLO (3, J2)

This cavernous Gothic church (San Zanipolo in Venetian), founded by the Dominicans and completed in 1430, rivals the Franciscans' Frari (p14) in size and grandeur. The similarities between the two, such as the use of brick and the red-and-white marble chequerboard floor inside, are evident.

INFORMATION

☎ 041 523 59 13
✉ Campo SS Giovanni e Paolo, Cannaregio
€ €2.50
🕐 9.30am-7pm Mon-Sat, 1-7pm Sun
🚇 Ospedale Civile
♿ limited
🍴 Osteria al Ponte (p57)

The interior is divided into an enormous central nave and two aisles, separated by graceful, soaring arches. A **stained-glass window** made in Murano in the 15th century (restored in the 1980s) fills the southern arm of the transept with light. A host of artists contributed to the window's design, including Vivarini, Cima da Conegliano and Girolamo Mocetto. Below the window and just to the right is a fine **pala** (altarpiece) by Lorenzo Lotto. On the opposite aisle wall, below the organ, is a triptych by Bartolomeo Vivarini. Noteworthy, too, are the five late-Gothic apses. Look out for Giovanni Bellini's polyptych of St Vincent Ferrer (San Vincenzo Ferreri) over the second altar of the right aisle.

In the **Cappella del Rosario**, off the northern arm of the transept, is a series of paintings by Paolo Veronese, including ceiling panels and an *Adorazione dei Pastori* (Adoration of the Shepherds).

Bragadin Bites the Dust

When the Turks took Famagusta (Cyprus) in 1570, they reserved a special fate for the Venetian commander, Marcantonio Bragadin. Having lopped off his nose and ears and left him to rot for a couple of weeks, his captors skinned him alive. One account says he only passed out when they reached his waist. The corpse was beheaded and the skin stuffed and sent to Constantinople. His remains, stolen in 1596, lie in SS Giovanni e Paolo.

Sights & Activities

MUSEUMS & GALLERIES

Ca' Rezzonico – Museo del Settecento Veneziano (3, D5)

Designed by Longhena and completed in the 1750s, this magnificent mansion houses a collection of 18th-century art (including some fine ceiling frescoes by Tiepolo) and period furniture. It is also worth visiting for the views over the Grand Canal. The Salone da Ballo (ballroom) drips with frescoes and is richly furnished with 18th-century couches, tables and statues in ebony.

☎ 041 241 01 00
🖥 www.museicivicien eziani.it ✉ Fondamenta Rezzonico, Dorsoduro 3136 € adult/student/ child €6.50/4.50/2.50
🕐 10am-6pm Wed-Mon Apr-Oct, 10am-5pm Wed-Mon Nov-Mar
🚤 Ca' Rezzonico 🚹 good

Fondaco dei Turchi (3, D1)

A domineering 19th-century façade hides a fine 12th- and 13th-century building, where in the 17th century the Turkish

All's well in the cloisters of Museo Diocesano d'Arte Sacra

trading community took up residence. Inside is the now partially reopened **Museo Civico di Storia Naturale** (Natural History Museum), whose odder displays include a dinosaur skeleton, the remains of 12m-long prehistoric crocodile skeleton and a tiny aquarium dedicated to Venetian coastal specimens.

☎ 041 275 02 06
🖥 www.museicivicien eziani.it ✉ Salizzada del Fondaco dei Turchi, Santa Croce 1730 € free
🕐 10am-6pm Sat & Sun
🚤 Riva de Biasio or San Stae 🚹 good

Museo Correr (3, H5)

Housed in the Ala Napo-leonica, or Napoleonic wing, the museum is dedicated to the art and history of Venice, with everything from 19th-century paintings, books, and documents to model galleys, maps and weaponry. Attached is the **Museo Archeologico**, crammed mostly with Greek and Roman statuary, and the Libreria Nazionale Marciana, with its 16th-century **Sala della Libreria** decorated by artists including Veronese.

☎ 041 240 52 11
🖥 www.museicivicien eziani.it ✉ Piazza San Marco, San Marco 52

Well, Well, Well

In days gone by, Venice had far fewer bridges and no running water, but an ingenious well system. Nowadays sealed shut, you'll see the wells in almost every square.

Each well is surrounded by as many as four depressions up to 4m away. Rainwater drained into these depressions and seeped into a cistern below. Sand or gravel inside the cistern acted as a filter. In the middle of the cistern, a brick cylinder (the well) extended to the bottom. The cistern itself was sealed off with impenetrable clay to keep salt water out.

Museo Archeologico

€ adult/student & EU senior €11/5.50 (incl Palazzo Ducale, Museo Archeologico Nazionale & Biblioteca Nazionale Marciana) ⏰ 9am-7pm Apr-Oct, 9am-5pm Nov-Mar 🚤 San Marco & Vallaresso ♿ fair

Museo della Fondazione Querini-Stampalia (3, J3)

The inside of this *palazzo* (mansion) features some surprising modern touches by the Venetian architect Carlo Scarpa. The museum contains furniture, personal effects and mostly minor art held by the Querini family. Look out for Giovanni Bellini's *Presentazione di Gesù al Tempio* (Presentation of Jesus at the Temple) and Gabriele Bella's curious scenes of Venetian life.
☎ 041 271 14 11
💻 www.querinistampalia.it ✉ Ponte Querini, Castello 4778 **€** adult/student & senior €6/4 ⏰ 10am-6pm Tue-Thu & Sun, 10am-10pm Fri & Sat 🚤 San Zaccaria ♿ limited

Museo delle Icone (2, F4)

Attached to San Giorgio dei Greci (p29), this gallery is dedicated to Orthodox religious art. On display are some 80 works of art and other items. Foremost are two 14th-century Byzantine icons, one representing Christ in Glory and the other the Virgin Mary with Child and Apostles. Many were created by Greeks in Venice and northern Italy.
☎ 041 522 65 81
💻 www.istitutoellenico.org ✉ Campiello dei

Greci, Castello 3412
€ adult/student €4/2
⏰ 9am-12.30pm & 1.30-4.30pm Mon-Sat, 9am-5pm Sun 🚤 San Zaccaria

Museo Diocesano d'Arte Sacra (3, J4)

The most interesting element of this religious art museum is the charming Romanesque cloister, a rarity in Venice and often open longer hours than the art display itself, which is housed in a former Benedictine monastery dedicated to Sant'Apollonia.
☎ 041 522 91 66
✉ Fondamenta di Sant'Apollonia, Castello 4312 **€** voluntary contribution ⏰ 10.30am-12.30pm Mon-Sat 🚤 San Zaccaria

Museo Storico Navale (2, G5)

Spread over four floors in a former grain silo, this museum traces the maritime history of the city and of Italy. Models abound of everything from the *bucintoro* (the *doges'* ceremonial barge) to WWII battleships. Up on the third floor is a room containing a few gondolas, including Peggy Guggenheim's.
☎ 041 520 02 76
✉ Fondamenta dell'Arsenale, Castello 2148 **€** €1.55 ⏰ 8.45am-1.30pm Mon-Fri, 8.45am-1pm Sat 🚤 Arsenale

Palazzo Fortuny (3, F4)

Sporting two rows of *hectafores*, each a series of eight connected Venetian-style windows, this mansion

Museo Storico Navale

was bought by Mariano Fortuny y Madrazo, an eccentric Spanish painter and collector, in the early 20th century. His works, and another 80 by the Roman artist Virgilio Guidi, make up the display. It is still undergoing restoration and opens for temporary exhibitions only.
☎ 041 520 09 95
💻 www.museicivicoveneziani.it ✉ Campo San Beneto, San Marco 3780
€ adult/student €4/2.50
⏰ 10am-6pm Tue-Sun 🚤 Sant'Angelo

Telecom Future Centre (3, G3)

Set up in the 15th-century cloisters of the adjacent Chiesa di San Salvador (p30) and nerve centre of the city's telephone services, this museum of the future shows us how we might communicate decades from now – a little science faction fantasy in the heart of the venerable historic city.
☎ 041 521 32 00
💻 www.futurecentre.telecomitalia.it
✉ Campo San Salvador, San Marco 4826 **€** free ⏰ 10am-6pm Tue-Sun 🚤 Rialto

NOTABLE BUILDINGS & MONUMENTS

Arsenale (2, G4)

Venice's huge dockyards were founded in 1104 and churned out warships and merchantmen on an industrial scale. The area is still navy property but parts have been taken over by the Biennale to stage exhibitions throughout much of the year.

✉ **Campo del'Arsenale, Castello 2407** € **depends on exhibition** ⌚ **depends on exhibition** 🚇 **Arsenale**

Ateneo Veneto (3, F5)

This learned society, founded in Napoleon's time, was once the headquarters of the confraternity of San Girolamo and Santa Maria della Giustizia, whose main task was to accompany criminals on death row in their last moments. The building was known as the Scuola 'dei Picai' (the old Venetian version of Dead Men Walking).

✉ **Campo San Fantin, San Marco** 🚇 **Vallaresso & San Marco** ♿ **limited**

Bartolomeo Colleoni Statue (3, J2)

Presiding over the Campo SS Giovanni e Paolo is by far the most impressive of the city's two equestrian statues. Created by the Florentine Verrocchio (1435–88), the statue is dedicated to the *condottiero* Bartolomeo Colleoni (1400–76), who from 1448 commanded mercenary armies in the name of the Republic.

✉ **Campo SS Giovanni e Paolo, Castello** 🚇 **Ospedale Civile**

Ca' Foscari (3, D4)

This late-Gothic structure was commissioned by Doge Francesco Foscari and is now the seat of the university. Although one of the finest mansions in the city, it has fallen into disrepair. In mid-1999 a deceptively realistic mock façade was unveiled to hide restoration work that is still underway.

✉ **Campiello de Ca' Foscari, Dorsoduro 3246** 🚇 **San Tomà**

Casa di Goldoni (3, D4)

Venice's greatest playwright, Carlo Goldoni (1707–93) was born in the Palazzo Centani, which is now better known as his house. It has been opened up as a museum, although there is little to see but some 18th-century marionettes and a series of images of, and commentaries on, the playwright (in Italian only).

☎ **041 275 93 25**
✉ **Calle Nomboli, San Polo 2794** € **adult/child €2.50/1.50** ⌚ **10am-5pm Mon-Sat Apr-Oct, 10am-4pm Mon-Sat Nov-Mar** 🚇 **San Tomà** ♿ **good**

Dogana da Mar (3, G6)

The customs offices that long occupied the low slung Dogana have long gone. The Punta della Dogana marks the split between the Grand Canal and the Canale della Giudecca. Atop the Dogana da Mar buildings are two bronze Atlases and above them turns capricious Fortune, an elaborate weather vane. Like sea

A Mercenary Moved

When freewheeling mercenary Bartolomeo Colleoni died in 1474, he bequeathed 216,000 gold and silver ducats and considerably more in property to his former employer, the city of Venice, on condition that a statue to him be raised in Piazza San Marco. Venice took the money and also raised the statue, a masterpiece as it happens, but could not stomach the idea of having it in the city's main square. Instead, la Serenissima opted to place it in Campo SS Giovanni e Paolo, which, after all, is fronted by the Scuola Grande di *San Marco*!

DAMIEN SIMONIS

water churned by the prow that is Punta della Dogana rises a striking modern steel and Murano glass sculpture from the lagoon. Two curved 'wings' rising 5m are topped by polychrome slivers of Murano glass that together perform a scintillating light show on the water.

✉ **Punta della Dogana, Dorsoduro 10** 🚤 **Salute** ♿ **good**

Find out how other half lived in 18th-century Venice

Fondaco dei Tedeschi (3, G2)

From the 13th century, the German business community occupied this *fondaco* (trading house). The present building was raised after a fire in 1505, and decorated by Giorgione and Titian (see also Ca' d'Oro p20). The courtyard was covered in 1937 and the building now serves as a post office.

✉ **Salizzada del Fondaco dei Tedeschi, San Marco 5346** 🕒 **8.30am-6.30pm Mon-Sat** 🚤 **Rialto** ♿ **good**

Ospedaletto (2, F4)

Longhena's 17th-century 'Little Hospital' (aka Chiesa di Santa Maria dei Derelitti) was the focal point of a former hospital for elderly and poor patients. It remains one of the gaudiest displays of baroque in Venice. In an annexe is the elegantly frescoed Sala da Musica, where patients performed concerts.

☎ **041 271 90 12** ✉ **Barbaria delle Tole, Castello 6691** 💶 **€2 (Sala da Musica)** 🕒 **3.30-6.30pm Thu-Sat** 🚤 **Ospedale Civile**

Palazzo Contarini del Bovolo (3, G4)

Built in the late 15th century, the Contarini mansion is nicknamed after its dizzying external spiral (*bovolo* in the Venetian dialect) staircase. The building maintains a hint of the Gothic in its arches and capitals. You can enter the grounds if you wish, although the staircase is quite visible from outside.

☎ **041 271 90 12** ✉ **Calle Contarini del Bovolo, San Marco 4299** 💶 **adult/child €2.50/2** 🕒 **10am-6pm** 🚤 **Rialto** ♿ **limited**

Palazzo Dario (3, F6)

The best way to appreciate this *palazzo* is from the No 1 *vaporetto* – the unique Renaissance marble facing was taken down and re-attached in the 19th century.

The place is supposed to be cursed as several of its owners have died sudden deaths down the years.

✉ **Calle Barbaro, Dorsoduro 352** 🚤 **Salute**

Palazzo Mocenigo (3, E1)

Once the property of one of the Republic's most important families, the mansion now houses a modest museum featuring period clothes, furnishings and accessories of the 18th century. This is how the other half lived in the twilight years of la Serenissima.

☎ **041 72 17 98** 🖥 **www.museicivici veneziani.it** ✉ **Salizzada di San Stae, Santa Croce 1992** 💶 **adult/child €4/2.50** 🕒 **10am-5pm Tue-Sun Apr-Oct, 10am-4pm Tue-Sun Nov-Mar** 🚤 **San Stae**

Cheapskate Republic

When Titian and Giorgione turned up at the Palazzo Ducale to pick up their payment of 150 ducats for the Fondaco dei Tedeschi frescoes, they were told their work was only worth 130 ducats. After insisting on an independent appraisal, which confirmed the figure of 150 ducats, they were still only offered 130 ducats – take it or leave it. Titian increasingly took commissions from abroad!

Palazzo Vendramin-Calergi (4, D3)
Gamblers approaching by water taxi *(motoscafo)* are greeted by the restrained Renaissance façade of what is now home to the city casino (see also p65). The composer Richard Wagner died here in 1883. You can wander into the ground floor area but must pay to see the gaming rooms. To tour the rooms Wagner occupied you must book a place on Friday between 10am and noon for the tour that takes place at 10.30am on Saturday.
☎ 041 529 69 90
✉ Campiello Vendramin, Cannaregio 2040 € free
🕑 3.30pm-2.30am Oct-May (gaming rooms); 10.30am Sat (guided tour) 🚊 San Marcuola
♿ limited

Scuola di San Giorgio degli Schiavoni (2, F4)
Venice's Dalmatian community established this religious school in the 15th century. On the ground floor the walls are graced by a series of superb paintings by Vittore Carpaccio depicting events in the lives of the three patron saints of

A Lopsided Look
Making a good gondola is no easy task – seven different types of wood are employed to make 280 pieces for the hull alone, which *must* be asymmetrical. The left side has a greater curve to make up for the lateral action of the oar, and the cross section is skewed to the right to counterbalance the weight of the gondolier.

Dalmatia: George, Tryphone and Jerome. The image of St George dispatching the dragon to the next life is particularly graphic.
☎ 041 522 88 28 ✉ Calle dei Furlani, Castello 3259/a € €3 🕑 9.30am-12.30pm & 3.30-6.30pm Tue-Sat, 9.30am-12.30pm Sun Apr-Oct, 10am-12.30pm & 3-6pm Tue-Sat, 10am-12.30pm Sun Nov-Mar 🚊 San Zaccaria ♿ limited

Scuola Grande dei Carmini (3, B5)
In its heyday, this was probably the most powerful of Venice's religious confraternities, with a membership in 1675 of 75,000. The façades have been attributed to Longhena. Of its numerous works of art, the nine ceiling paintings by Tiepolo in the

Salone Superiore (upstairs) depict the virtues surrounding the Virgin in Glory.
☎ 041 528 94 20 ✉ Rio Terrà Canal, Dorsoduro 2617 € adult/student €5/4 🕑 9am-6pm Mon-Sat, 9am-4pm Sun Apr-Oct, 9am-4pm Nov-Mar 🚊 Ca' Rezzonico ♿ limited

Squero di San Trovaso (3, C6)
On the leafy banks of the Rio di San Trovaso, one of Venice's most attractive waterways, you can see one of the few working *squeri* (gondola workshops) left in the city. From the right bank, look across to the vessels in various states of (dis)repair in the timber worksheds.
✉ Campo San Trovaso, Dorsoduro 1097
🚊 Zattere

CHURCHES & CATHEDRALS

Cattedrale di San Pietro di Castello (2, H5)
This isolated post-Palladian cathedral, with the gleaming but leaning bell tower, is the latest successor to a long line of churches that have stood here since 775. Although it was Venice's cathedral until 1807, for centuries it had been

bridesmaid to the Basilica di San Marco.
✉ Isola di San Pietro, Castello € €2.50 or Chorus ticket 🕑 10am-5pm Mon-Sat, 1-5pm Sun 🚊 San Pietro

Gesuati (2, D5)
Also known as the Chiesa di Santa Maria del Rosario,

this 18th-century Dominican church contains ceiling frescoes by Tiepolo telling the story of St Dominic. The statues lining the interior are by Gian Maria Morlaiter (1699–1781).
☎ 041 523 06 25 ✉ Fondamenta Zattere ai Gesuati, Dorsoduro 918 € €2.50 or Chorus ticket

⏱ 10am-5pm Mon-Sat, 1-5pm Sun 🚤 Zattere ♿ limited

I Gesuiti (2, E3)

The Jesuits took over this church in 1657 and reconstructed it in Roman baroque style. Inside the lavish décor includes white and gold stucco, white and green marble floors and flourishes filling empty slots. Remarkable paintings found here are Tintoretto's *Assunzione della Vergine* (Assumption of the Virgin), and Titian's *Martirio di San Lorenzo* (Martyrdom of St Lawrence).

☎ 041 528 65 79
✉ Campo dei Gesuiti, Cannaregio 4885 € free
⏱ 10am-noon & 4-6pm
🚤 Fondamente Nuove
♿ limited

Madonna dell'Orto (4, E1)

This 14th-century church was raised after a statue of the Virgin Mary was discovered by 'miracle' in a nearby garden. Mostly Gothic, the church has some Romanesque touches as well as later changes. The statues crowning the façade were added in the 18th century. You'll find the famous white Madonna statue in the Cappella di San Mauro.

✉ Campo della Madonna dell'Orto, Cannaregio 3520 € €2.50 or Chorus ticket ⏱ 10am-5pm Mon-Sat, 1-5pm Sun
🚤 Madonna dell'Orto
♿ limited

San Francesco della Vigna (2, F4)

The first glimpse of this powerful Palladian façade comes as a shock. The church itself was designed by Sansovino for the Franciscans on the site of a vineyard. The bell tower could be the twin of St Mark's Campanile. Inside, the Cappella dei Giustiniani, left of the main altar, is decorated with splendid reliefs by Pietro Lombardo and his school.

✉ Campo San Francesco della Vigna, Castello 2787 € free ⏱ 8am-12.30pm & 3-7pm
🚤 Celestia ♿ limited

San Giacomo dell'Orio (3, D1)

Built to replace a 9th-century church (in 1225), this is one of the few decent examples of Romanesque in Venice. The main Gothic addition (14th century) is the remarkable wooden ceiling. Among the intriguing jumble inside you'll find a 13th-century baptismal font, a Byzantine column in green marble and a rare work by Lorenzo Lotto, *Madonna col Bambino e Santi* (Madonna with Child and Saints).

✉ Campo di San Giacomo dell'Orio, Santa

An intriguing jumble at San Giacomo dell'Orio

Croce € €2.50 or Chorus ticket ⏱ 10am-5pm Mon-Sat, 1-5pm Sun
🚤 Riva de Biasio
♿ limited

San Giorgio dei Greci (2, F4)

Here in 1526 Greek Orthodox refugees were allowed to raise a church. It is interesting for the richness of its Byzantine icons, iconostasis and other works inside. Visit the Museo delle Icone next door (p25).

☎ 041 522 54 46
✉ Campiello dei Greci, Castello 3412 € free
⏱ 9am-1pm & 3-4.30pm Mon & Wed-Sat, 9am-1pm Sun 🚤 San Zaccaria

---

Tintoretto Treasure

A big draw at the Chiesa della Madonna dell'Orto are the frescoes by Tintoretto, who was a local parishioner. Among them are the *Giudizio Finale* (Last Judgment), *Adorazione del Vitello d'Oro* (Adoration of the Golden Calf) and the *Apparizione della Croce a San Pietro* (St Peter's Vision of the Cross). On the wall at the end of the right aisle is the *Presentazione di Maria al Tempio* (Presentation of the Virgin Mary in the Temple). Tintoretto is buried with other family members in the church.

San Polo (3, E3)

Largely obscured by the housing tacked on to it, you'd never know this church is of Byzantine origin. Inside, a whole cycle by Tiepolo, the *Via Crucis* (Stations of the Cross) is on view.

✉ Campo San Polo, San Polo 2118 € €2.50 or Chorus ticket ⏱ 10am-5pm Mon-Sat, 1-5pm Sun 🚊 San Silvestro ♿ limited

San Salvador (3, G3)

Built on a plan of three Greek crosses laid end to end, this church is among the city's oldest, although the present façade was erected in 1663. Among the noteworthy works inside is Titian's *Annunciazione* (Annunciation). Behind the main altar is his *Trasfigurazione* (Transfiguration).

☎ 041 523 67 17 🖥 www.chiesasansal vador.it ✉ Campo San Salvador, San Marco 4835 € free ⏱ 9am-noon & 3-6pm Mon-Sat Apr-Oct, 9am-noon & 4-6pm Mon-Fri Nov-Mar 🚊 Rialto ♿ limited

Busy baroque at San Stae

The very ornate pediment of Santa Maria del Giglio

San Sebastian (3, A6)

What you see here is the Renaissance reconstruction of Paolo Veronese's parish church. Veronese decorated the inside with frescoes and canvases that cover much of the ceiling and walls. The organ is his work too, with scenes from Christ's life on its shutters. Titian contributed his *San Nicolò*, on the right as soon as you enter.

✉ Campo San Sebastiano, Dorsoduro € €2.50 or Chorus ticket ⏱ 10am-5pm Mon-Sat, 1-5pm Sun 🚊 San Basilio ♿ limited

San Stae (3, E1)

The busy baroque façade of this church dedicated to St Eustace (San Stae) belies the simple interior. Among its art treasures are Tiepolo's *Il Martirio di San Bartolomeo* (the Martyrdom of St Bartholomew). Next door, to the left (No 1980), is the **Scuola dei Tiraoro e Battioro**, the former seat of the goldsmith confraternity's *scuola*.

✉ Campo San Stae, Santa Croce 1979 € €2.50 or Chorus ticket ⏱ 10am-5pm Mon-Sat, 1-5pm Sun 🚊 San Stae ♿ limited

San Zaccaria (2, F5)

Construction of this church started in Gothic (see the apses) but ended in Renaissance. On the second altar to the left after you enter is a startlingly vivid image of the Virgin Mary by Giovanni Bellini. The Cappella di Sant'Atanasio holds some Tintorettos and Tiepolos. The vaults of the Cappella di San Tarasion are covered in frescoes.

☎ 041 522 12 57 ✉ Campo San Zaccaria, Castello 4693 € free; Cappella di Sant'Atanasio €1 ⏱ 10am-noon & 4-6pm Mon-Sat, 4-6pm Sun 🚊 San Zaccaria ♿ limited

Sant'Alvise (2, D2)

Built in 1388, the church hosts a noteworthy Tiepolo, the *Salita al Calvario* (Climb to Calvary), a distressingly human depiction of one of Christ's falls under the weight of the cross. The

ceiling frescoes are an unexpected riot of colour.
✉ **Campo Sant'Alvise, Cannaregio 3205**
€ **€2.50 or Chorus ticket**
☺ **10am-5pm Mon-Sat, 1-5pm Sun** ⚓ **Sant'Alvise**
♿ **limited**

Santa Maria dei Miracoli (3, H2)

And well might one speak of *miracoli* (miracles). Pietro Lombardo was responsible for this Renaissance jewel, which is fully carapaced inside and out in marble, bas-reliefs and statues. The timber ceiling is also eye-catching. Pietro and Tullio Lombardo executed the carvings on the choir.
✉ **Campo dei Miracoli, Cannaregio 6074**
€ **€2.50 or Chorus ticket**
☺ **10am-5pm Mon-Sat, 1-5pm Sun** ⚓ **Rialto**
♿ **limited**

Santa Maria del Giglio (3, F5)

The baroque façade of this place (aka Santa Maria Zobenigo) features maps of European cities and hides the fact that a church has stood here since the 10th century. A small affair, it is jammed with paintings, such as Peter Paul Rubens' *Madonna col Bambino e San Giovanni* (his only work in Venice).
✉ **Campo Santa Maria Zobenigo, San Marco 2543** € **€2.50 or Chorus ticket** ☺ **10am-5pm Mon-Sat, 1-5pm Sun**
⚓ **Santa Maria del Giglio**
♿ **limited**

Santa Maria Formosa (3, J3)

Rebuilt in 1492 on the site of a 7th-century church, the name Santa Maria Formosa stems from the legend behind the church's initial foundation. San Magno, bishop of Oderzo, is said to have had a vision of the Virgin Mary on this spot. In this instance she was *formosa* (beautiful, curvy). Inside is an altarpiece by Palma il Vecchio depicting St Barbara.
✉ **Campo Santa Maria Formosa, Castello 5254**
€ **€2.50 or Chorus ticket**
☺ **10am-5pm Mon-Sat, 1-5pm Sun** ⚓ **San Zaccaria** ♿ **limited**

Santo Stefano (3, E5)

One of only three churches in Venice to have been attached to a convent,

Teeming with Tintorettos: Santo Stefano

Santo Stefano boasts the finest timber ceiling of any church in Venice. In the museum right of the altar is a collection of Tintorettos, including the *Ultima Cena* (Last Supper) and *Lavanda dei Piedi* (Washing of the Feet). The bell tower has a serious lean.
✉ **Campo Santo Stefano, San Marco 3825** € **free; museum €2.50 or Chorus ticket** ☺ **10am-5pm Mon-Sat, 1-5pm Sun**
⚓ **Accademia** ♿ **limited**

SS Redentore (2, E6)

The authorities ordered Palladio to design this grand church in thanksgiving for the passing of the plague in 1577. It was finished by Antonio da Ponte. Inside are a few works by Tintoretto, Veronese and Vivarini, but it is the powerful theatrical façade that most inspires observers.
✉ **Campo del SS Redentore, Giudecca 94**
€ **€2.50 or Chorus ticket**
☺ **10am-5pm Mon-Sat, 1-5pm Sun** ⚓ **Redentore**
♿ **limited**

Pontoon Pilgrims

On the third Saturday of July each year, a grand pontoon bridge is created from all sorts of boats tied together between the Zattere (from outside Spirito Santo) and Chiesa del SS Redentore, allowing the citizens of Venice to make a pilgrimage that their forebears first undertook in 1578. Many people hang about on the boats with friends to party and watch the fireworks that night. The Festa del Redentore (Feast of the Redeemer) remains one of the city's prime celebrations.

BRIDGES, CAMPI & PUBLIC SPACES

Biennale Internazionale d'Arte (2, H5)

The pavilions of the Biennale (Arsenale, p26) form a mini-compendium of 20th-century architectural thinking. Carlo Scarpa worked often on the Italian Pavilion and built the Venezuelan one (1954). Also look for the Padiglione del Libro (Book Pavilion; 1991), Dutch Pavilion (1954), Austrian Pavilion (1934) and Australian Pavilion (1988).

✉ **Biennale Internazionale d'Arte, Castello** 🏛 **Giardini** ♿ **good**

Campo Santa Margherita (3, C4)

A real people's square, this space takes on a truly living air in the afternoon as kids come out to play and the youth of Venice sip *spritzes*

Brave Venetians eat gelato in white trousers

A pigeon's view of Piazza San Marco

(p63) at the many bars and cafés. The squat little object at the square's southern end was one of the city's many religious *scuole*.

✉ **Campo Santa Margherita, Dorsoduro** 🏛 **Ca' Rezzonico** ♿ **limited**

Campo Santa Maria Formosa (3, J3)

One of Venice's most appealing squares, this is full of local life. Among the ageing mansions, **Palazzo Vitturi** is a good example of the Veneto–Byzantine style, while the **Palazzi Donà** are a mix of Gothic and late Gothic.

✉ **Campo Santa Maria Formosa, Castello** 🏛 **San Zaccaria** ♿ **limited**

Giardini Papadopoli (3, A2)

These gardens, one of the few green spaces open to the public, were a great

deal more impressive until 1932, when the Rio Nuovo was slammed through them.

✉ **Fondamenta del Croce, Santa Croce** € **free** 🕐 **8am-7.30pm summer, 8am-5.30pm winter** 🏛 **Piazzale Roma** ♿ **good**

Piazza San Marco (3, H5)

The belly button of Venice, the square is fronted by the basilica and other emblematic buildings like the Procuratie Nuove, the Procuratie Vecchie, the Ala Napoleonica (with the Museo Correr, p24), the Torre dell'Orologio (clock tower) and **Campanile** (adult/child €6/3; 🕐 9am-9pm late Jun-Aug, 9am-7pm Apr-Jun & Sep-Oct, 9am-4pm Nov-Mar), the Basilica's freestanding bell tower, from the top of which you can enjoy breathtaking views.

✉ **Piazza San Marco, San Marco** 🏛 **Rialto** ♿ **limited**

Ponte di Calatrava (3, A2)

A rare flash of modernity is being added to the Venetian cityscape with

An Evening with Veronica

Veronica Franco, one of the city's best remembered courtesans, lived on Campo Santa Maria Formosa. Poet, friend of Tintoretto and lover of France's King Henry III, Miss Franco's costly services ranged from witty discourse to horizontal folk dancing.

Santiago Calatrava's bridge, a fantasy of glass, stone and steel that is being built to link Piazzale Roma with the train station – a work of modern art in progress, you might say.

✉ **Ponte di Calatrava, Santa Croce/Cannaregio** 🚊 **Piazzale Roma or Ferrovia**

Ponte dei Scalzi (3, B1)

This elegant high-arched bridge is the first of the three (soon to be four) across the Grand Canal. Built in 1934, it replaced an iron bridge built by the Austrians in 1858.

✉ **Ponte dei Scalzi, Cannaregio/Santa Croce** 🚊 **Ferrovia**

Ponte dell'Accademia (3, E6)

Built in timber in 1930 to replace a 19th-century metal structure, the third and last of the Grand Canal bridges was supposed to be a temporary arrangement. From the middle, the views both ways up the Grand Canal are spellbinding.

✉ **Ponte dell'Accademia, Dorsoduro/San Marco** 🚊 **Accademia**

Ponte delle Guglie (4, B2)

So-called because of the *guglie* (little obelisks) at either end, this is the main crossing point over the Canale di Cannaregio, and there probably isn't a tourist who doesn't cross it en route from the train station to Piazza San Marco.

✉ **Ponte delle Guglie, Cannaregio** 🚊 **Guglie** ♿ **good**

Ponte delle Tette (3, E2)

Tits Bridge got its name around the late 15th century because prostitutes around here tended to display their wares to encourage business. Beyond the bridge is Rio Terrà delle Carampane. The name came from a noble family's house (Ca' Rampani), and at some point the ladies of the night who loitered here also came to be known as *carampane*.

✉ **Ponte delle Tette, San Polo** 🚊 **San Stae**

Ponte di Rialto (3, G3)

For centuries the only bridge over the Grand Canal was here, linking the Rialto with San Marco. Antonio da Ponte (Anthony of the Bridge) completed this robust marble version in 1592, at a cost of 250,000 ducats. It had been preceded by several timber bridges and a wobbly pontoon arrangement as far back as 1180.

✉ **Ponte di Rialto, San Polo/San Marco** 🚊 **Rialto**

Sant'Elena (2, H5)

Housing construction began in 1925 in this, the quietest and leafiest residential corner of Venice. The arrival of riot police and armies of football supporters at the **Stadio Penzo** are a bit of a weekend jolt. The humble Gothic **Chiesa di Sant'Elena** is just past the stadium.

✉ **Sant'Elena** 🚊 **Sant'Elena** ♿ **good**

Bridge of the little obelisks

The Oldest Profession

In the 1530s, Venice had about 11,000 registered prostitutes of a population of 120,000. Attitudes towards the profession changed with each generation, but in the late 15th century a city ordinance stipulated that ladies of the night should hawk bare-breasted. It appears that la Serenissima was concerned that its men were increasingly turning to sodomy. Fearing for Venetian manhood, prostitution was encouraged and sodomy made punishable by death.

ISLANDS

Giudecca (2, B6–F6)

Lying flat out like a long outer sea wall south of Venice, the tranquil island of Giudecca is thought to have been an early medieval home to the city's Jews. Later Venice's big-name families had grand holiday properties here, replaced in the 19th century by factories, boatyards and prisons. The main attractions are Palladio's Chiesa del SS Redentore (p31) and the Cipriani hotel complex.
✉ **Giudecca** 🚊 **Sacca Fisola, Redentore & Zitelle**

Le Vignole (5, E2)

The southwest of Le Vignole is owned by the military and contains an old fort, the Forte Sant'Andrea, which

Where did I leave my clothes?

may only be seen from the sea. The island long produced the bulk of the *doge's* wine and its 50 or so inhabitants still live mainly from agriculture.
✉ **Le Vignole** 🚊 **Vignole** ♿ **limited**

Lido (5, E3)

On summer weekends Venetians flock to the beach here and in September

SS Maria e Donato: two saints are better than one

celebs from all over crowd in to the **Palazzo della Mostra del Cinema** for the Venice film festival (see p62). At the north end of this long island is the **Antico Cimitero Israelitico** (former Jewish cemetery), which can be visited by organised tour – ask at the Museo Ebraico (p17).
✉ **Lido** 🚊 **Lido** ♿ **limited**

Murano (2, G1)

The people of Venice have been making crystal and glass since the 10th century. The bulk of the industry was moved to Murano in 1291 and production methods were a closely guarded secret. Look out for glassworks along Fondamenta

Row Your Boat

Back in 1882 the **Reale Società Canottieri Bucintoro** (☎ 041 520 56 30; www.bucintoro.org; Dorsoduro 15; 1yr membership €170; office ⏱ 3.30-5.30pm Tue, 10am-noon Sat) was established by royal concession. Inspired by the English rowing fraternities of Oxbridge, the club furnished Italy with Olympic champions (the entire gold medal team at the 1952 Olympics were Bucintoro members). Now the oldest rowing club in Venice, Bucintoro boasts about 300 members of all ages, types and sizes. Outsiders are welcome to join. Even rank beginners can have a go at learning to row, either *voga veneta* (the local standing version) or the classical sit-down style known here as *voga inglese* (English rowing). There's no better way to navigate the lagoon!

dei Vetrai and Viale Garibaldi. The **Museo Vetrario** (2, H1; ☎ 041 73 95 86; Fondamenta Giustinian 8; adult/child €4/2.50 ☒ 10am-5pm Thu-Tue Apr-Oct, 10am-4pm Thu-Tue Nov-Mar) has some exquisite pieces. The **Chiesa dei SS Maria e Donato** (2, H1; Campo San Donato; free; ☒ 9am-noon & 3.30-7pm Mon-Sat, 3.30-7pm Sun) is a fascinating example of Veneto-Byzantine architecture.

☒ **Murano** ☀ **Murano Colonna, Museo or Faro** ♿ **limited**

Pellestrina (1, D3)

Pellestrina stretches south like an 11km-long razor blade from the Lido to Chioggia. Small villages made up of farming and fishing families are spread out along the island, protected on the seaward side by the Murazzi (sea walls), a feat of 18th-century engineering. Long grey sand beaches separate the Murazzi from the sea on calm days.

☒ **Pellestrina** ☀ **Lido & No 11 bus** ♿ **limited**

San Francesco del Deserto (5, F1)

The Franciscans built a monastery on this island 1km south of Burano to keep away from it all. Legend says Francis of Assisi himself landed here. Malaria and other hardships obliged the Franciscans to leave in 1420. Pope Pius II subsequently granted the island to another order, the **Minori Osservanti** (☎ 041 528 68 63; donation encouraged

Getting Down to Chioggia

The most important town in the Comune di Venezia after Venice and a big fishing port, Chioggia lies at the south of the lagoon. Wander along Corso del Popolo, visit the Chiesa di San Domenico for Vittore Carpaccio's *San Paolo* and check out the fish market. Get the *vaporetto* to the Lido and then switch to the No 11 bus, which heads down to Chioggia via two car ferries and Pellestrina.

☒ 9-11am & 3-5pm Tue-Sun), which remains here.
☒ **San Francesco del Deserto** ☀ **water taxi from Burano** ♿ **limited**

San Lazzaro degli Armeni (5, D3)

In 1717 the Armenian Mechitarist fathers were handed this former leper colony. They founded a monastery and an important centre of learning. Visitors can see the 18th-century refectory, church, library, museum and **art gallery** (☎ 041 526 01 04; adult/child €6/3; ☒ guided tour only 3.25-5pm). A mix of Venetian and Armenian art is on show, along with a room dedicated to Lord Byron, who frequently stayed on the island.

☒ **San Lazzaro degli Armeni** ☀ **San Lazzaro** ♿ **limited**

San Michele (2, F2)

Napoleon established this island cemetery away from the city for health reasons. The **Chiesa di San Michele in Isola** was among the city's first Renaissance buildings. Ezra Pound, Sergei Diaghilev and Igor Stravinsky are pushing up daisies here, in the

Mosaic detail at cemetery

'acatholic' sections (signposted) to the northeast of the island.

☒ **San Michele** € **free** ☒ **7.30am-4pm Oct-Mar, 7.30am-6pm Apr-Sep** ☀ **Cimitero** ♿ **limited**

Sant'Erasmo (5, F2)

Together with Le Vignole, Sant'Erasmo was long known as the *orto di Venezia* (Venice's Garden) and its 1000 inhabitants remain largely dedicated to rural pursuits. Apart from green fields, quiet settlements and a couple of summertime restaurants, you can see the **Torre Massimiliana**, a 19th-century Austrian defensive fort in the southeast.

☒ **Sant'Erasmo** ☀ **Capannone, Chiesa & Punta Vela** ♿ **limited**

VENICE FOR CHILDREN

Art and architecture might not keep the kids amused for long but there is plenty of interesting activity on the city's waterways. A gelato (ice cream) at strategic intervals also works wonders. You cannot avoid the bridges so leave prams at home and invest in a baby backpack.

Giardini Pubblici (2, H6)
The most extensive public park in Venice is a trifle tatty, but it's better than nothing and you will find swings and things to amuse the little ones. A handy restaurant/bar with outdoor seating completes the picture.
✉ **Giardini Pubblici, Castello** 🚊 **Giardini** ♿ **fair**

Gondola Rides
Once the standard means of getting around town, these strangely shaped vessels remain for many the quintessence of romantic Venice. They are as enchanting for wide-eyed kids as starry-eyed lovers! You can hire them for tours or even as taxis if you have lots of cash. Try to bargain the price down if you can.
☎ **041 520 06 85 San Marco, 041 522 49 04**

Voluptuous sculpture in the Giardini Pubblici

Rialto, 041 522 11 51 Piazzale Roma, 041 71 85 43 Stazione di Santa Lucia € €62 for 50 min before 8pm, €77.50 after 8pm

Lido Beaches (5, E3)
To escape the summer swelter take the kids to the beach. This involves a soothing ferry ride to the Lido and then either walking to nearby pay beaches or getting a bus or rental bicycles to look for free beaches further south (such as at Alberoni).
✉ **Lido** € **€5-9 to rent sun-lounges on some beaches** 🚊 **Lido** ♿ **good**

Parco Savorgnan (4, B2)
You'd hardly know this quiet, well hidden park existed unless directed there.

It is a fairly small affair but has a few swings and diversions for the wee bairns and can come as a welcome relief from the chaos in the railway station area.
☎ 041 521 70 11 ✉ **Fondamenta Savorgnan, Cannaregio** 🕐 8am-5.30pm Oct-Mar, 8am-7.30pm Apr-Sep 🚊 **Guglie** ♿ **good**

Vaporetto No 1
This one really is a must for all the family. Hop aboard the all stops No 1 *vaporetto* from your arrival point (for most this is the train station or Piazzale Roma) and chug along the Grand Canal. It's a trip kids aged one to 100 can do time and again without getting bored.
🚊 **No 1** ♿ **limited**

Escape the swelter on the beach at Laguna

For Kids of All Ages
- Museo Storico Navale (p25)
- Campanile (p32)
- Telecom Future Centre (p25)

Out & About

WALKING TOURS

Rambling to the Rialto

Start by the **Chiesa dei SS Giovanni e Paolo** (**1**; p23) and the **Scuola Grande di San Marco** (**2**). Pass below the statue of **Bartolomeo Colleoni** (**3**; p26) as you cross the bridge and head west for the **Chiesa di Santa Maria dei Miracoli** (**4**; p31). From its entrance proceed southeast across the Rio di San Marina and swing westwards – you will see the **Teatro Malibran** (**5**) as you make for the **Chiesa di San Giovanni Crisostomo** (**6**) before turning south past the grim-looking **Fondaco dei Tedeschi** (**7**; p27) for **Campo San Bartolomeo** (**8**). After saluting Goldoni's statue go west for Venice's emblematic bridge, the **Ponte di Rialto** (**9**; p33), which leads to the area of the same name.

Once the financial hub of Venice, it is a crush of activity as people flock to the markets. On your right is the Renaissance **Palazzo dei Camerlenghi** (**10**) and just beyond that the **Chiesa di San Giacomo di Rialto** (**11**). To your left is the **Palazzo dei Dieci Savi** (**12**; Palace of the Ten Wise Men). In its shadow stands the **Fabbriche Vecchie** (**13**). Passing the **Fabbriche Nuove** (**14**) you finish at the 700-year-old **Pescaria** (**15**; Fish Market; p49), rebuilt in 1907. Pop into **All'Arco** (p54) for some traditional snack refreshment.

> **distance** 1.2km **duration** 40min
> ▶ **start** 🚊 Ospedale Civile
> ● **end** 🚊 Ca' d'Oro

If you get tired of walking, take a gondola

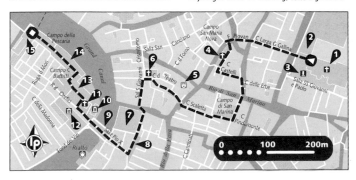

Bridge to Bridge

Start atop the high-arched **Ponte dei Scalzi** (**1**; p33) and take in the views over the Grand Canal before crossing into Santa Croce, where you will pass the grand stone iconostasis that marks the entrance to the **Scuola**

Ponte dell'Accademia in Campo San Vidal

Grande di San Giovanni Evangelista (**2**). Cross Campo San Stin and two bridges to reach the impressive Gothic hulk of the **Chiesa di Santa Maria Gloriosa dei Frari** (**3**; p14) and, around the corner, the wedding-cake façade of **Scuola Grande di San Rocco** (**4**; p15), with its Tintoretto feast. Continuing south, you skirt the **Chiesa di San Pantalon** (**5**) en route to the lively **Campo Santa Margherita** (**6**; p32), where you could halt for a *spritz* at **Margaret Duchamp** (p64). Check out the Tiepolos in the **Scuola Grande dei Carmini** (**7**; p28), and the **Chiesa dei Carmini** (**8**), before crossing the canal south and heading east for the **Chiesa di San Barnaba** (**9**). From here, follow Calle di Toletta and cross the Rio di Trovaso to arrive at the **Gallerie dell'Accademia** (**10**; p12). Right in front you can climb the **Ponte dell'Accademia** (**11**; p33) to enjoy one of Venice's most famous views.

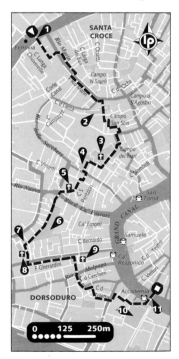

distance 2km **duration** 1hr
▶ **start** 🚊 Ferrovia
⏺ **end** 🚊 Accademia

Between Cathedrals

This takes us from the city's cathedral, the Basilica di San Marco, to the church it usurped in that role, San Pietro. Begin at **Piazza San Marco** (**1**; p32), where you could while away hours. Turn into Piazzetta di San Marco and pass between the statue-symbols of Venice, St Theodore and St Mark (represented by the lion). Turn east. On the first bridge look north to the **Ponte dei Sospiri** (**2**; Bridge of Sighs) and then duck up Calle degli Albanesi for the **Museo Diocesano d'Arte Sacra** (**3**; p25) and its Romanesque cloister. Head east along Salizzada San Provolo to the **Chiesa di San Zaccaria** (**4**; p30), from whose square you return to the waterfront.

Ponte dei Sospiri: somewhere in there behind the bride

The lagoonside stroll takes you past **Chiesa della Pietà** (**5**), Vivaldi's church, and on to the **Museo Storico Navale** (**6**; p25) and, nearby, the once mighty shipyards of the **Arsenale** (**7**; p26). Back by the water, swing inland along Castello's main drag, Via G Garibaldi, where you plunge into local life and could stop for a drink in one of the cafés, before dropping south through the **Giardini Pubblici** (**8**; p36). Sidle north alongside residential Sant'Elena and back to Via G Garibaldi. Proceed to the **Cattedrale di San Pietro di Castello** (**9**; p28) on the eponymous island.

distance 4.2km **duration** 2½hr
▶ **start** 🚊 Vallaresso, San Marco & San Zaccaria
◉ **end** 🚊 San Pietro

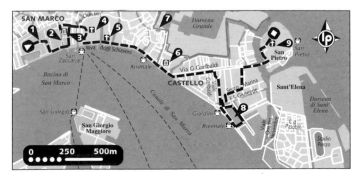

DAY TRIPS
Padua (1, C2)

A medieval university town, Padua is a treasure chest of art, too. The nucleus of old Padua is formed by Piazza delle Erbe and Piazza della Frutta, busy market squares separated by the majestic **Palazzo della Ragione** (€8; 9am-7pm Tue-Sun). The frescoed *salone* on the first floor is magnificent. Pilgrims flock to the **Basilica del Santo** (or di Sant'Antonio; Piazza del Santo 6.30am-7pm), which houses the tomb and relics of the town's patron saint (St Anthony). A different kind of pilgrimage has art-lovers streaming in to behold the vision of Giotto's fresco cycle in the **Cappella degli Scrovegni** (049-201 00 20; www.cappelladegliscrovegni.it; Giardini dell'Arena; €11/4, booking required; 9am-10pm). Completed in 1306, the cycle presages the creative explosion of the Renaissance.

INFORMATION
37km west of Venice
- Padua; up to 40min
- € PadovaCard (€14) for all main sights
- ℹ tourist office (049-876 79 27; Vicolo Pedrocchi & at the train station)
- ✕ Per Bacco (049-875 46 64; Piazzale Pontecorvo 10)

Bang in the middle of the market; Palazzo della Ragione

Vicenza (1, B2)

Vicenza flourished as Roman Vicentia and fairly bristles with the architectural handiwork of Renaissance genius Palladio. He began work on the **Basilica Palladiana** (0444-32 36 81; Piazza dei Signori; 9am-5pm Tue-Sun) in 1549 over an earlier Gothic building. Among his mansions are **Palazzo Barbaran da Porto** (0444-32 30 14; ContràPorti 11; €5; 10am-6pm Tue-Sun), **Palazzo Isoppo da Porto** at No 21 and the classic **La Rotonda** (0444-32 17 93; Via Rotonda; €6; 10am-noon & 3-6pm Wed Mar-Nov), inspiration for the White House and other neoclassical gems in the Anglo-Saxon world.

The **Teatro Olimpico** (0444-22 28 00; Corso Andrea Palladio; €7; 9am-5pm Tue-Sun Sep-Jun, 9am-7pm Tue-Sun Jul-Aug), was designed by Palladio and Vincenzo Scamozzi and is a superb example of Renaissance architecture.

INFORMATION
72km west of Venice
- Vicenza; 50min
- ℹ tourist office (0444-32 08 54; Piazza Matteotti 12 & 0444-32 70 72; Piazza dei Signori)
- ✕ Il Cursore (0444-32 35 04; Stradella Pozzetto 10)

Verona (1, A2)

Shakespeare thought the blood feuds of medieval Verona so intriguing he wrote a blockbusting play about them, *Romeo and Juliet*. The Veronese in turn were no slouches, and so 'little Rome' has for centuries also been sold to romantics as the city of Romeo…and Juliet. You can even see her house, the **Casa di Giulietta** (☎ 045-803 43 03; Via Cappello 23; €3.10; 🕙 8.30am-7.30pm Tue-Sun, 1.30-7.30pm Mon). Pity she didn't exist!

A great deal more real is the pink marble, 1st-century AD **Roman Arena** (☎ 045-800 32 04; Piazza Brà; €3.10; 🕙 9am-7pm Tue-Sun, 1.45-7.30pm Mon, 8am-3.30pm during opera season), third largest Roman amphitheatre in existence. It does a roaring trade as Verona's summer open-air opera house.

Originally the site of a Roman forum, **Piazza delle Erbe** remains the lively heart of the city today. It is lined with sumptuous buildings, including the baroque **Palazzo Maffei**, at the north end, with the adjoining 14th-century **Torre del Gardello**. On the east flank is the frescoed **Casa Mazzanti**, a

INFORMATION
120km west of Venice
🚆 Verona; 1hr 35min
ℹ️ tourist office (☎ 045-806 86 80; Via degli Alpini 9)
✖️ Bottega del Vino (☎ 045-800 45 35; Vicolo Scudo di Francia 3/a)

former residence of the medieval ruling della Scala family. Ascend the nearby 12th-century **Torre dei Lamberti** (by elevator €2.10, on foot €1.50; 🕙 9am-6pm Tue-Sun) for the views.

The mantle of Verona is studded with the jewels of fine churches (combined ticket €5, admission to each €2). Seek out in particular the 12th-century **cathedral** (Piazza del Duomo; 🕙 10am-5.30pm Mon-Sat, 1.30-5.30pm Sun), which combines Romanesque (lower section) and Gothic (upper section) styles. Others worth a look are **Chiesa di Sant' Anastasia** (Piazza di Sant'Anastasia), **Chiesa di San Fermo** (Stradone San Fermo), and the **Basilica di San Zeno Maggiore** (Piazza San Zeno 2).

Painted palazzo in *piccola Roma*

ORGANISED TOURS

Many museums such as the Palazzo Ducale (p10) organise guided tours at a price. The **Museo Archeologico** and **Libreria Nazionale Marciana** offer free tours. For details of both, see under the listing 'Museo Correr' on p24.

Local travel agencies can put you on to city tours ranging from two-hour guided walks for €27 to gondola rides with a serenade for €35 per person. One such agency is **Agenzia Kele & Teo** (3, H4; ☎ 041 520 87 22; San Marco 4930).

Basilica di San Marco Mosaics (3, J4)
The Patriarcato (church body in Venice) organises guided tours of the mosaics in St Mark's Basilica. You are given a detailed explanation of their biblical significance. The timetable can vary, so call ahead to be sure.
☎ 041 270 24 21
✉ Piazza San Marco, San Marco € free
☻ English: 11am Mon, Thu, Fri; French: 11am Thu; Italian: 11am Mon-Tue & Thu-Sat

Città d'Acqua (Cities on Water; 5, B1; Officina Viaggi)
The Maree Veneziane tours explore various parts of the lagoon, including the Arsenale (otherwise virtually impossible to visit), Malamocco (5, B2), Le Vignole (5, E2) and Giudecca.
☎ 041 93 68 33
💻 www.veniceitineraries .com ✉ Centro Internazionale Città d'Acqua,

> ## I Want to Be Alone!
> Want to be guided but remain alone? Pick up a 'My Venice' handheld audio set from the tourist office in the Venice Pavilion (3, H5; 2 days €15, per hr €3). With the accompanying map, you can follow commentated itineraries to key parts of the city. Want a break? Switch it off!

Officina Viaggi, Via Col Moschin 14, Mestre
€ per person up to €75 (minimum group of 40), per person up to €95 (group of 10-39)
☻ variable (minimum 10 people required)

Magic & Enchantment of Venetian Life (3, G5; American Express office)
You are guided through the streets of the Sestiere di San Marco and then across the Grand Canal by gondola to visit the Frari (p14). It's then on to the Rialto by gondola along back canals.
☎ 041 520 08 44
✉ American Express,

Salizzada San Moisè, San Marco 1471 € 2½hr English-language tour €35
☻ Apr-Oct 3pm

RiViviNatura (3, E5)
This group organises offbeat day tours around the lagoon in anything from large traditional *bragozze* under sail to a *vaporetto*. Call ahead. It might not always be easy to get English-language guides.
☎ 041 277 41 89
💻 www.rivivinatura.it
✉ Calle dei Vitturi, San Marco 2923 € per person up to €50

Venetian Legends
Manuel Vecchina leads a 1½-hour evening walk based on tales and legends of ghosts and other shiver-inducing types. He bases his walk on Alberto Toso Fei's *Venetian Legends and Ghost Stories* (www.venetianlegends.it).
☎ 348-341 83 92 € per person €20

Mosaic in the Basilica di San Marco

Shopping

Venice offers the ardent shopper endless scope for maxing out credit cards. If classic Venetian items such as Murano glass, Burano lace, marbled paper and Carnevale masks don't do it for you, a host of other options, from high Italian fashion to curious handicrafts, will surely entice.

Shopping Areas

In Venice, the main shopping area for clothing, shoes, accessories and jewellery is in the narrow streets between Piazza San Marco (3, H5) and the Rialto (3, G2), particularly the Mercerie and around Campo San Luca (3, G4). The more up-market shops are west of Piazza San Marco.

For Carnevale masks, costumes, ceramics and model gondolas, **San Polo** (3) is the best hunting ground. Another Venetian speciality, marbled paper, is found all over town. **Murano** glass can be obtained on the island (2, G1) or in shops mainly in the San Marco area. Lace, another speciality, is most easily bought on the island of **Burano** (5, F1), although several shops in Venice also sell it.

Tax Refunds

A value-added tax of about 19%, known as IVA, is slapped onto just about everything in Italy. If you are resident outside the EU and spend more than €155 in the same shop on the same day, you can claim a refund on this tax when you leave the EU. The refund only applies to purchases from affiliated retail outlets that display a 'Tax free for Tourists' sign. You have to complete a form at the point of sale, then get it stamped by Italian customs as you leave. At major airports you can get an immediate cash refund.

Opening Hours

Store opening hours are about 9.30am to 7.30pm, with a two-hour break from 1pm or 1.30pm. Bigger stores and increasingly some small shops skip the lunch break. However, treat the hours given in this chapter with caution – often the final arbiter is the whim of the shop owner. Most shops open Saturday and some, anxious to attract every tourist euro, on Sunday too. Several shops shut through at least part of August.

Fancy some lace? If you don't have time to visit Burano, try San Marco

ART

The single biggest concentration of galleries, selling a variety of art, is the Dorsoduro area on the streets that lie between the Gallerie dell'Accademia (3, D6) and the Peggy Guggenheim Collection (3, E6), as well as along Calle del Bastion (3, F6). Calle delle Carrozze (3, D5) and surrounding streets in San Marco are also worth a look.

BAC Art Studio (3, E6)
This studio has paintings, aquatints and engravings by Cadore and Paolo Baruffaldi which can make fine gifts. Cadore concentrates his commercial efforts on street and canal scenes, while Baruffaldi mainly depicts masked people. There are also quality postcards.
☎ 041 522 81 71
✉ Campo San Vio, Dorsoduro 862 ⏰ 10am-1pm & 3-7pm Mon-Sat
🚤 Accademia

Bugno Art Gallery (3, F5)
This luxury gallery has some works by contemporary artists on permanent display, although sales are the primary objective. While you might not be able to afford a Mirò or De Chirico, there's plenty of other

material for the modern art collector.
☎ 041 523 13 05
✉ Campo San Fantin, San Marco 1996/a
⏰ 10.30am-12.30pm & 4-7.30pm Tue-Sat, 4-7.30pm Sun-Mon
🚤 Santa Maria del Giglio

Galleria Ferruzzi (2, D5)
Ferruzzi's images of Venice are an engaging, almost naïve distortion of what we see. With fat brush strokes and primary colours, the artist creates a kind of children's gingerbread Venice. You'll find screen prints, paintings and postcard versions.
☎ 041 520 59 96
✉ Fondamenta Zorzi Bragadin, Dorsoduro 523 ⏰ 10am-6.30pm
🚤 Accademia

Galleria Traghetto (3, F5)
A stalwart on the Venetian art scene, this is one of the most respected of the few Venetian galleries dealing in contemporary artists, mostly Italian but open to international flavours.
☎ 041 522 11 88
✉ Calle di Piovan, San Marco 2543 ⏰ 10.30am-12.30pm & 3.30-7.30pm Mon-Sat 🚤 Santa Maria del Giglio

Artwork by Vincenzo Eulisse at Bugno Gallery

ANTIQUES & CRAFTS

A Mano (3, D3)
This shop is full of all sorts of decorative items and all goods are handmade. Quirky lampshades, mirrors and a host of other gewgaws certainly make it an interesting stop for some window shopping.
☎ 041 71 57 42 ✉ Rio Terrà, San Polo 2616 ⏰ 10am-1.30pm & 2.30-7.30pm Tue-Sat 🚤 San Tomà

Antiquus (3, E5)
This inviting little shop boasts a solid collection of old masters, silverware and antique jewellery. Alongside the few items of furniture sit grand tea sets and other aristocratic bric-a-brac.
☎ 041 520 63 95
✉ Calle delle Botteghe, San Marco 3131 ⏰ 3.30-7.30pm Mon, 10am-12.30pm & 3.30-7.30pm Tue-Sun 🚤 San Samuele

Arca (3, E1)
The designs in this eye-catching shop are powerful, and for some tastes the colours are possibly even a little strong. Teresa della Valentina paints her tiles and a variety of other ceramic objects in bold, bright, deep hues.
☎ 041 71 04 27 ✉ Calle del Tintor, Santa Croce 1811 ⏰ 9.30am-7.30pm 🚤 San Stae

Gilberto Penzo (3, D3)
Here you can buy exquisite hand-built wooden models of various Venetian vessels. Mr Penzo also takes in old ones for restoration. For the kids, snap up the gondola model kits.
☎ 041 71 93 72 ✉ Calle Saoneri, San Polo 2681
🕑 9.30am-12.30pm & 3-6pm Mon-Sat
🚉 San Tomà

Jesurum (3, H3)
Michelangelo Jesurum opened a lace school on Burano in 1860 and 18 years later the island women's work won the firm a prize at a Universal Exposition. It remains one of the quality names in Burano lace.
☎ 041 520 60 85
✉ Merceria del Capitello, San Marco 4856
🕑 9.30am-7.30pm Mon-Sat, 10am-1pm & 2-7pm Sun 🚉 Rialto

Laboratorio del Gervasuti (2, F5)
In this higgledy-piggledy workshop are enough goods to whet the appetite of any antiques collector, but if you are a serious purchaser ask to see the warehouse.
☎ 041 523 67 77
✉ Campo Bandiera e Moro, Castello 3725
🕑 10am-4.30pm
🚉 San Zaccaria

La Margherita Ceramiche (3, F2)
Margherita Rossetto's kitchen pots, clocks and other hand-painted items are all tranquil designs in soft blues and yellows.
☎ 041 72 31 20
✉ Sotoportego de Siora

Gilberto's Gondolas

Gilberto Penzo long ago became passionate about gondolas. He began to build models and collect detailed plans of them and all other lagoon and Adriatic vessels. He founded an association aimed at keeping all this ancient knowledge fresh, and to finance it all he opened a shop (left).

Bettina, Santa Croce 2345
🕑 10am-6pm Mon-Fri, 10am-1pm Sat
🚉 San Stae

Livio de Marchi (3, E5)
This place, with wooden sculptures of underpants, socks and shirts, is rather strange but endearing all the same. Just what you might do with a fine carving of an unironed shirt in your living room remains unclear.
☎ 041 528 56 94 ✉ Salizzada San Samuele, San Marco 3157/a 🕑 9am-noon & 2-6pm Mon-Fri
🚉 San Samuele

Valese (3, H4)
Since 1918 the Valese family has been casting figures in bronze and other metals. Its reputation is unequalled in the city. Not all the items might suggest themselves as souvenirs, but the horses that adorn the flanks of the city's gondolas are tempting.
☎ 041 522 72 82
✉ Calle Fiubera, San Marco 793 🕑 9.30am-7pm Mon-Sat 🚉 Vallaresso & San Marco

Gilty pleasures

Ripped Off?

Feel you've been had? Received lousy service? You could try leaving a complaint at one of the tourist offices or calling the dedicated complaints service on ☎ 041 529 87 10. There may be little they can do to redress a wrong, but this is not to say they will not try in more outrageous cases. If nothing else, it'll allow you to let off some steam.

BOOKS & MUSIC

Editore Filippi (3, J4)
Don't let the unremarkable appearance fool you. This is a den of books on all manner of subjects related to Venice, many published and sold exclusively here. The Filippis have been in the business for nearly a century. Scholars search them out for their encyclopaedic knowledge.
☎ 041 523 56 35
✉ Calle Casselleria, Castello 5763 🕑 9am-12.30pm & 3-7.30pm Mon-Sat 🚊 San Zaccaria

Libreria al Ponte (3, F4)
This small but useful shop offers a solid range of guides and other books on Venice, as well as children's books, many in English. It stocks Donna Leon's mystery detective yarns too.
☎ 041 522 40 30
✉ Calle della Cortesia, San Marco 3717/d
🕑 9.30am-9.15pm Mon-Sat 🚊 Rialto

Librairie Française (2, F4)
Voulez-vous vos livres en français? Here you will find everything from the latest bestsellers of Gallic literature to a plethora of titles on all subjects Venetian – the lot of it in French.
☎ 041 522 96 59
✉ Barbaria de le Tole, Castello 6358 🕑 3.30-7pm Mon, 9am-12.30pm & 3.30-7pm Tue-Sat 🚊 Ospedale Civile

Mille e Una Nota (3, F3)
If during your stay in Venice you require strings for your guitar, or would like to acquire some new panpipes, a shiny new mouth organ or perhaps even a harp, this is the place to visit.
☎ 041 523 18 22
✉ Calle del Mezzo, San Polo 1235 🕑 9.30am-1pm & 3-7.30pm Mon-Sat 🚊 San Silvestro

Peggy Guggenheim Museum Shop (3, E6)
Located in the same building as the gallery of the same name (but with a different entrance), the shop offers a select array of coffee-table books and souvenirs related mostly to the gallery's modern-art collections.
☎ 041 240 54 24
✉ Fondamenta Venier dai Leoni, Dorsoduro 710
🕑 10am-6pm Wed-Mon
🚊 Accademia

San Marco Studium (3, J4)
Just off Piazza San Marco, this shop, with books piled high and wide, stocks a broad offering of English-language guides and books on Venice. It has material in other languages too.
☎ 041 522 23 82
✉ Calle de la Canonica, San Marco 337/a 🕑 9am-7.30pm Mon-Sat 🚊 San Zaccaria

Vivaldi Store (3, H3)
Looking for a Vivaldi or Albinoni CD? This is your place. Cristiano Nalesso specialises in all things musically Venetian, from the Renaissance through to baroque.
☎ 041 522 13 43 ✉ Salizzada del Fontego dei Tedeschi, San Marco 5537
🕑 9.30am-7pm Mon-Sat, 1-7pm Sun 🚊 Rialto

CARNEVALE MASKS & COSTUMES

Atelier Pietro Longhi (3, D3)
Ever fancied a helmet and sword to go with your tailor-made Carnevale costume? Maybe a Harlequin outfit, or just a top hat? This is one of the classic costume stores.
☎ 041 71 44 78 ✉ Rio Terrà, San Polo 2604/b
🕑 10am-12.30pm & 3-7pm Mon-Fri, 10am-12.30pm Sat 🚊 San Tomà

Ca' Macana (3, C5)
Wander in and watch the artists at work on the raw papier-mâché of future masks in this, one of the better mask-makers in the city.
☎ 041 520 32 29
✉ Calle delle Botteghe, Dorsoduro 5176 🕑 10am-6.30pm Sun-Fri, 10am-8pm Sat 🚊 Ca' Rezzonico

L'Arlecchino (3, F2)
Here they claim the masks are made only with papier-mâché to their own designs. To prove it you can inspect their workshop and see production from the earliest phases to the finishing

touches. The quality of masks is evident.

☎ 041 71 65 91 ✉ Calle dei Cristi, San Polo 1722-1729 🕑 9.30am-7.30pm 🚉 San Silvestro

Mondonovo Maschere (3, C5)

Like many other shops in Venice, this workshop and boutique doesn't seem much from the outside, but one of the city's master mask-makers, Guerrino Lovato, is behind it all. He was commissioned to provide the masks for Stanley Kubrick's *Eyes Wide Shut*.

☎ 041 528 73 44 🖳 www.mondonovo maschere.it ✉ Rio Terrà Canal, Dorsoduro 3063 🕑 9am-1.30pm & 2.30-7pm Mon-Sat 🚉 Ca' Rezzonico

Tragicomica (3, D3)

One of the bigger mask and costume merchants, Tragicomica also organises costume parties during Carnevale. The place is quite overwhelming at first sight.

☎ 041 72 11 02 ✉ Calle Nomboli, San

Polo 2800 🕑 10am-1.30pm & 2.30-7pm 🚉 San Tomà

Tragicomica mask

FOOD & DRINK

Aliani (3, F2)

For an outstanding assortment of cheeses and other delicatessen products, Aliani has long been a favoured stop in the Rialto. You will also find a range of wines and other products.

☎ 041 522 49 13 ✉ Ruga Vecchia di San Giovanni, San Polo 654 🕑 8am-1pm & 5-7.30pm Mon-Sat 🚉 Rialto

Caffè Costarica (4, C2)

Since 1930 the Marchi family has been importing coffee from Costa Rica and other coffee-producing countries. It is toasted daily for your delectation. Or you can sip some at the bar.

☎ 041 71 63 71 ✉ Rio Terrà San Leonardo, Cannaregio 1337 🕑 8am-1pm & 3.30-7.30pm Mon-Sat 🚉 San Marcuola

Drogheria Mascari (3, G2)

The Drogheria Mascari is another Venetian foodies' classic. Jars of goods, salty and sweet, are accompanied by a mouth-watering range of sweets, including slabs of chocolate and nougat.

☎ 041 522 97 62 ✉ Ruga degli Spezleri, San Polo 381 🕑 8am-1pm & 4-7.30pm Thu-Tue, 8am-1pm Wed, 🚉 Rialto

GLASS & CRYSTAL

Barovier & Toso (2, G2)

Your chequebook will tremble as you enter this temple of artistic glassware. The displays allow you to appreciate top glass creations, perhaps better to observe than acquire.

☎ 041 527 43 85 🖳 www.barovier .com ✉ Fondamenta dei Vetrai 28, Murano 🕑 10am-12.30pm & 1-6pm Mon-Sat 🚉 Colonna

Berengo (2, G1)

Here is a purveyor of glass that has long abandoned any pretence at functionality in its products. This is glass for art's sake. If you are into the idea of glass as sculpture, this is an interesting stop.

☎ 041 527 63 64 🖳 www.berengo.com ✉ Fondamenta dei Vetrai 109/a, Murano 🕑 10am-6pm 🚉 Colonna

Berengo glass sculpture

L'Isola (3, G5)
Carlo Moretti designs a range of functional and decorative glass items, often boasting

Oozing elegance at l'Isola

deeply primary colours and always oozing elegance.
☎ 041 523 19 73
✉ Campo San Moisè, San Marco 1468 🕑 9am-1pm & 3.30-7.30pm Mon-Sat
🚇 Vallaresso & San Marco

Marco Polo (2, G2)
One of the handful of large and reliable glass merchants in Murano, Marco Polo offers you the opportunity to see the masters at work and see a display of traditional glassware; you can also have objects tailor-made and sent to your country. Upstairs is a museum of contemporary glass with names from local master Andres Pagnes to interna-

tional creators like Tony Cragg or Costas Varotsos.
☎ 041 73 99 04
🖥 www.marcopologlass.it ✉ Fondamenta Manin 1, Murano 🕑 9am-6pm Mon-Sat 🚇 Colonna

Venini (2, G1)
Venini is another top-shelf name in artistic glassware and crystal. It also has a branch in central Venice (3, H4; ☎ 041 522 40 45; Piazzetta dei Leoni, San Marco 314).
☎ 041 73 99 55
🖥 www.venini.it
✉ Fondamenta dei Vetrai 47-50, Murano 🕑 9.30am-5.30pm Mon-Sat 🚇 Colonna

CLOTHING, SHOES & ACCESSORIES

Codognato (3, G5)
Possibly the city's best known jewellery shop, Codognato has classic pieces that have attracted the likes of Jackie Onassis. Hours tend to be capricious.
☎ 041 522 50 42 ✉ Calle Seconda dell'Ascensione, San Marco 1295 🕑 4-7pm Mon, 10am-1pm & 4-7pm Tue-Sun 🚇 Vallaresso & San Marco

Fiorella Gallery (3, E5)
You'll find all sorts of odd billowing and fantastical clothing items here. They adorn striking transsexual doge mannequins scattered about the inside and windows of this unique store.
☎ 041 520 92 28
✉ Campo Santo Stefano, San Marco 2806 🕑 10am-7pm Mon-Sat 🚇 Accademia

Clothing as sculpture

Fashionable Retail Therapy
Fashion fiends should head for the streets around and just west of Piazza San Marco, where they will find ranks of stores that generally open seven days. These include:
- **Armani** (3, G4; ☎ 041 523 78 08; Calle dei Fabbri 989)
- **Fendi** (3, G5; ☎ 041 520 57 33; Salizzada San Moisè 1474)
- **Gucci** (3, G5; ☎ 041 241 39 68; Calle Larga XXII Marzo 2102)
- **Prada** (3, G5; ☎ 041 528 39 66; Salizzada San Moisè 1464-1469)
- **Salvatore Ferragamo** (3, G5; ☎ 041 277 85 09; Calle Larga XXII Marzo 2093)
- **Versace** (3, G5; ☎ 041 520 00 57; Campo San Moisè 1462)

CLOTHING & SHOE SIZES

Women's Clothing

Aust/UK	8	10	12	14	16	18
Europe	36	38	40	42	44	46
Japan	5	7	9	11	13	15
USA	6	8	10	12	14	16

Women's Shoes

Aust/USA	5	6	7	8	9	10
Europe	35	36	37	38	39	40
France only	35	36	38	39	40	42
Japan	22	23	24	25	26	27
UK	3½	4½	5½	6½	7½	8½

Men's Clothing

Aust	92	96	100	104	108	112
Europe	46	48	50	52	54	56

Japan	S	M	M		L	
UK/USA	35	36	37	38	39	40

Men's Shirts (Collar Sizes)

Aust/Japan	38	39	40	41	42	43
Europe	38	39	40	41	42	43
UK/USA	15	15½	16	16½	17	17½

Men's Shoes

Aust/ UK	7	8	9	10	11	12
Europe	41	42	43	44½	46	47
Japan	26	27	27.5	28	29	30
USA	7½	8½	9½	10½	11½	12½

Measurements approximate only; try before you buy.

Il Grifone (3, B3)

A virtually décor-free shop front disguises this one-man leather workshop where you can get to grips with quality handmade bags, belts, wallets and other leather objects for quite reasonable prices.
☎ 041 522 94 52
✉ Fondamenta del Gaffaro, Dorsoduro 3516
☙ 10am-7.30pm Mon-Sat ⚱ Piazzale Roma

Manuela Calzature (3, F3)

This is a small shoe shop with a good range, including more expensive footwear that they make under their own name. Don't judge it by the cheap junk outside.
☎ 041 522 66 52
✉ Calle del Galizzi, San Polo 1046
☙ 9am-7.30pm
⚱ San Silvestro

Mazzon Le Borse (3, D4)

An unassuming workshop well known to Venetian shoppers, this place is good for handmade leather bags and accessories. The goods are top class and often better than many of the big names.
☎ 041 520 34 21
✉ Campiello San Tomà, San Polo 2807
☙ 9.30am-12.30pm & 3.30-7pm Mon-Sat
⚱ San Tomà

MARKETS

Pescaria (3, F2)

Underneath the neo-Gothic roof built at the beginning of the 20th century, the Pescaria (Fish Market) gets a mixed clientele of domestic shoppers and restaurateurs in search of ingredients for the day's menu. They have been selling fish here for 700 years.
✉ Pescaria, Rialto, San Polo ☙ 7am-2pm
⚱ traghetto from Campo Santa Sofia or vaporetto Rialto

Mercatino dei Miracoli (3, H2)

This is a bric-a-brac market that is held monthly in two adjacent squares. You can turn up all sorts of odds and ends, and the atmosphere is always fun. There are two sites, so make sure to wander all the way through the market (2, G5).
✉ Campo San Canciano & Campo Santa Maria Nova ☙ 2nd or 3rd weekend every month
⚱ Ca' d'Oro

Rialto Produce Markets (3, G2)

The raucous cries of vendors rise above the general hubbub as the canny shoppers of Venice rub shoulders with unsuspecting neophyte tourists. A local favourite is the humble artichoke, prized by Venetians. Buy yourself the makings of a picnic.
✉ Rialto, San Polo ☙ 7am-2pm ⚱ Rialto or traghetto from Campo Santa Sofia

PAPER & STATIONERY

Venice is noted for its *carta marmorizzata* (marbled paper), used for all sorts of things, from expensive gift wrap to book covers.

Il Papiro (3, E5)
A bright, spacious stationer, Il Papiro doesn't pretend to compete with the traditional paper shops. Among a fairly modest selection of such items you will also find a

Marmorizzata at Il Papiro

range of items from elegant envelopes to letter openers.
☎ 041 522 30 55
✉ Calle del Spezier, San Marco 2764 ☼ 10am-7.30pm Sun, 10.30am-7pm Mon-Sat ⚓ Santa Maria del Giglio

Il Pavone (3, E6)
The dominant colours (blues, reds and yellows) and motifs (floral shapes, cherubs and others) at Il Pavone change from one day to the next. The templates are applied equally to hand-printed paper as well as to ties and other objects. You can have T-shirts made here, too.
☎ 041 523 45 17
✉ Fondamenta Venier

dai Leoni, Dorsoduro 721
☼ 9.30am-1.30pm & 2.30-7.30pm
⚓ Accademia

Legatoria Polliero (3, D3)
A traditional exponent of the art of Venetian book-binding with (and without) marbled paper. You barely have room to stand in this den, with stacks of leather-bound books, paper-bound folders and all sorts of other stationery piled higgledy-piggledy high to the rafters.
☎ 041 528 51 30
✉ Campo dei Frari, San Polo 2995 ☼ 9.30am-1.30pm & 2.30-7.30pm Mon-Sat ⚓ San Tomà

FOR CHILDREN

Disney Store (3, G3)
All right, perhaps you'll think it's like mentioning McDonald's. Fact is, kids love Disney toys and this place may well save a failing parental relationship with little ones at a key moment during your Venetian sojourn.
☎ 041 522 39 80
✉ Campo San Bartolomeo, San Marco 5257 ☼ 9.30am-7.30pm ⚓ Rialto

Gilberto Penzo (3, D3)
See p45.

Il Baule Blu (3, D4)
Come here for a luxury bear. The owners of this shop

have turned cuddly bears into a business for aficionados. If you've brought your own along to Venice, you can rest easy knowing that the shop also operates a Teddy Hospital.
☎ 041 71 94 48
✉ Campo San Tomà, San Polo 2916/a
☼ 10am-12.30pm & 4-7.30pm Mon-Sat
⚓ San Tomà

Molin Giocattoli (3, H2)
Sitting by what locals call Toys Bridge (Ponte dei Giocattoli), this shop will attract kids with a yearning for something more titillating than Tintoretto. Want a model Ferrari or *vaporetto*?
☎ 041 523 52 85 ✉ Salizzada San Canciano, Cannaregio 5899 ☼ 9am-1.30pm & 3.30-7.30pm Mon-Sat ⚓ Rialto

It's Sale Time!
Time your visit to coincide with the sales and you may pick up some great bargains. Winter sales run from early January to mid-February and the summer sales run from July to early September. Look for the *saldi* signs.

Eating

Can one eat well in Venice? Ask an Italian and you may be greeted by a contemptuous snort. Dining out is doubtless more expensive than elsewhere in Italy, and palming off second-rate food to unwitting tourists seems to be a Venetian sport.

But plenty of places, from the modest *osteria* (traditional bar/restaurant) serving snacks and wine to the impeccable luxury of Harry's Bar, constitute a healthy exception to the rule. After all, they have the locals to satisfy too!

Among the most promising areas to scout around are the San Polo and Santa Croce districts between the Rialto and Campo San Giacomo dell'Orio. Further south in Dorsoduro, you'll discover all

La dolce vita in Venice

sorts of goodies around Campo Santa Margherita. Several interesting spots hover around where the districts of San Marco, Cannaregio and Castello meet. Beyond that, good eateries are fairly evenly scattered across the labyrinthine game board that is Venice.

A full meal consists of an *antipasto* (starter), followed by the *primo piatto*, usually pasta, risotto or soup, and a *secondo* of fish or meat. Venice is a seaside town and fish predominates. You generally order a *contorno* (side of vegetables or salad) separately. Meals finish with a *dolce* (dessert), gelato (ice cream) or fruit and *caffè*. You can often eat considerably more cheaply at lunch if you opt for a set menu.

Restaurants generally open for lunch (12.30pm to 3pm) but often stop taking orders after 2pm. Evening dining starts at 7.30pm with few places serving after 10.30pm.

For *cicheti* (bar snacks) and local wine Venetians traditionally seek out a *bacaro* or *osteria*. The latter can also be an inn offering a limited menu of simple food and house wines. A *trattoria* is traditionally a family-run, no-frills restaurant, while a *ristorante* was always a self-consciously more upmarket option. These terms can be used as a guide, but the distinction between them is increasingly blurred.

Sidestepping Bad Salad
Steer clear of restaurants along tourist thoroughfares (such as the Lista di Spagna) advertising impossibly cheap three-course menus. Touts and multilingual menus are also a sign you could be treated to sloppy, microwaved impersonations of food. Watch out for the tour groups scoffing tired salad and droopy pasta.

SAN MARCO

Ai Rusteghi (3, H3) $
Snack Bar
Pop in here for a great range in mini-*panini* with all sorts of fillings. It also offers good wines. There's nothing better than a cool drink or two and a couple of delicious little *panini* as a quick lunch-time snack.
☎ 041 523 22 05
✉ Calletta della Bissa, San Marco 5529 ◷ lunch & dinner Mon-Sat 🚉 Rialto

Enoteca Il Volto (3, F4) $$
Wine Bar
Near Campo San Luca, this spot has an excellent wine selection and a tempting array of snacks, which will no doubt induce you to hang about for more than one glass. It is a classic of the Venetian scene.
☎ 041 522 89 45
✉ Calle Cavalli 4081 ◷ lunch & dinner Mon-Sat, lunch Sun 🚉 Rialto

Harry's Bar (3, H5) $$$$
Restaurant/Bar
The Cipriani family, who started this bar in 1931, claims to have invented many Venetian specialities, including the Bellini cocktail. On the culinary side, they also claim the patent for *carpaccio* (very fine slices of raw meat). Toscanini, Chaplin, Hemingway and just about everyone who was anyone (and quite a few who were definitely no-one) have eaten (and drunk) here. See also the boxed text on p63.
☎ 041 528 57 77
✉ Calle Vallaresso 1323 ◷ lunch & dinner 🚉 Vallaresso & San Marco

Osteria al Bacareto (3, E4) $$
Osteria/Trattoria
The search for a good traditional *trattoria* in this corner of San Marco is over when you reach al Bacareto. Since it doubles as an *osteria*, you can opt for a plateful of *cicheti* with a glass of wine.
☎ 041 528 93 36
✉ Calle Crosera 3447 ◷ lunch & dinner Mon-Fri 🚉 San Samuele ♿

Osteria alla Botte (3, H3) $$
Osteria
This youthful backstreet *bacaro* (much the same thing as an *osteria*) near the Rialto bridge is ideal for *cicheti* and a glass or two of *prosecco* at the bar. You could also opt for simple sit-down meals. Finish off with a glass of strawberry-flavoured *fragolino* wine.
☎ 041 520 97 75
✉ Calle della Bissa 5482 ◷ lunch & dinner Mon-Wed, Fri & Sat, lunch Sun 🚉 Rialto

Osteria San Marco (3, G5) $$$
Venetian
Out of a tired, oldtime *osteria* a team of dynamic young people have created a modern dining area with a range of local cooking, and even the occasional land-going critter.
☎ 041 528 52 42
✉ Frezzeria 1610 ◷ lunch & dinner Mon-Sat 🚉 Vallaresso & San Marco

Ristorante da Ivo (3, G4) $$$$
Restaurant
A Venetian dining classic, at da Ivo you will have a choice of seafood, predictably the house speciality, and a selection of Venetian and Tuscan meat dishes, all washed down with a fine range of wines. The atmosphere is quietly elegant.
☎ 041 528 50 04
✉ Calle dei Fuseri 1809 ◷ lunch & dinner Mon-Sat 🚉 Rialto

Join the hordes at Harry's Bar

DORSODURO

Ai Gondolieri (2, D5) $$$$
Restaurant
Surrounded as it is by innumerable seafood restaurants, Ai Gondolieri comes as a welcome change for red-blooded carnivores. All mains are land-going critters (such as Angus steak, duck and liver). Dishes can be accompanied by a select offering of wine. If you opt for all courses you will bust the €50 mark.
☎ 041 528 63 96
✉ Fondamenta Ospedaleto 366 🕑 lunch & dinner Wed-Mon
🏛 Accademia

Lineadombra (2, E5) $$$
Venetian
Inside is a modest designer dining area stretching back from the bar beneath low-slung timber beams. On a sunny day, most opt for a shaded table on the greenery-lined pontoon over the water. The limited menu offers an even choice

DAMIEN SIMONIS

A Venetian dining classic

It's the Business
Need to do some serious business munching? Try:
- Al Covo (p58)
- Da Fiore (p54)
- Fiaschetteria Toscana (p56)
- Ristorante da Ivo (p52)
- Vecio Fritolin (p55)

of seafood, fish and meat dishes.
☎ 041 241 18 81
✉ Ponte dell'Umiltà 19 🕑 lunch & dinner Thu-Tue 🏛 Zattere

L'Incontro (3, C5) $$
Restaurant
Typical Sardinian fare is served at this intimate restaurant. Try specialities like *culurgiones* (big potato and mint filled pasta pockets doused in a tomato sauce) and suckling pig.
☎ 041 522 24 04
✉ Rio Terrà Canal 3062 🕑 lunch & dinner Tue-Sun 🏛 Ca' Rezzonico ♿

Osteria San Pantalon (3, C4) $$
Venetian
Students with an eye for good local grub crowd in here for no-nonsense Venetian fare, including

baccalà mantecato (mashed up cod prepared in garlic and parsley) and *sarde in saor* (sardines prepared in an onion marinade).
☎ 041 71 08 49
✉ Calle del Scaleter 3958 🕑 lunch & dinner Mon-Fri & dinner Sat 🏛 San Tomà

Ristorante La Bitta (3, C5) $$
Meat
The short menu is dominated by meat dishes, with veal, Angus steaks and similar carnivorous options in the lead. The bottle-lined dining room leads to an attractive internal courtyard. At the bar you'll find a few *cicheti* too.
☎ 041 523 05 31 ✉ Calle Lunga San Barnaba 2753/a
🕑 dinner Tue-Sat
🏛 Ca' Rezzonico

CASTELLO

Al Covo (2, F5) $$$$
Restaurant
Cooking at Al Covo is resolutely local and of a high quality. Inside, the atmosphere is hushed and unpretentious. You can choose to eat meat and vegetable dishes *a la carta* or go for one of two seafood tasting-menus (€63 for seven courses or €78 for 10).
☎ 041 522 38 12
✉ Campiello della Pescaria 3968 ⏱ lunch & dinner Fri-Tue
🚊 San Zaccaria

Al Portego (3, H3) $$
Osteria
Situated beneath the portico that gives this *osteria* its name, Al Portego is an inviting stop for *cicheti* and wine, along with some robust meals. Try the *bigoli* (thick, rough Venetian pasta), and whatever sauce they come with.
☎ 041 522 90 38
✉ Calle Malvasia 6015

Sly Grog Shops
Want some no-nonsense plonk for a picnic? Do what the locals do and take an empty mineral-water bottle to a wine store for about €2 per litre! Here are a few of Nave de Oro's several branches:
- Rio Terrà San Leonardo, Cannaregio 1370 (4, C2)
- Calle dei SS Apostoli, Cannaregio 4657 (3, H1)
- Campo Santa Margherita, Dorsoduro 3664 (3, C4)
- Calle Mondo Nuovo, Castello 5786/b (3, J3)

⏱ lunch & dinner Mon-Sat 🚊 Rialto

Alle Testiere (3, J3) $$$$
Trattoria
The chef may well come for a chat as you sample the tasty offerings in the cosy dining area. Fish is the leitmotif. A handful of starters and pasta courses (all around €16) are followed by a couple of set mains or fresh fish. Round off with quality wines.
☎ 041 522 72 20
✉ Calle del Mondo Nuovo 5801 ⏱ lunch & dinner Tue-Sun 🚊 Rialto

Trattoria Corte Sconta (2, G4) $$$
Trattoria
A cosy eatery with the option of dining in the rear courtyard, Corte Sconta is well off even the unbeaten track. The chefs prepare almost exclusively seafood classics, such as their delicious *risotto ai scampi*. The owners claim to use only the catch of the day. Who can carp at such a policy? Try the homemade desserts.
☎ 041 522 70 24
✉ Calle Pestrin 3886
⏱ lunch & dinner Tue-Sat 🚊 Arsenale

Café Culture
Espresso – a small cup of strong black coffee
Doppio espresso – a double espresso
Caffè lungo – watery espresso (long black)
Caffè americano – approximation of filter coffee
Caffellatte – with milk, a breakfast coffee
Cappuccino – frothy version of a *caffellatte*, also a breakfast coffee
Caffè macchiato – espresso with a dash of frothy milk
Caffè freddo – a long glass with cold coffee and ice cubes
Corretto – espresso 'corrected' with grappa or other liquor

GIUDECCA

Ai Tre Scaini (2, E6) $$
Trattoria
In this rambunctious, and chaotic *trattoria* you can settle down with ebullient local families for no-nonsense pasta and seafood dishes. Throaty wine comes from a couple of small barrels set up inside. You can eat in the garden, too.

☎ 041 522 47 90 ✉ Calle Michelangelo 53/c ⏲ dinner Mon, lunch & dinner Tue-Wed & Fri-Sun ⚓ Zitelle ♿

Harry's Dolci (2, C6) $$$$
Restaurant/Snack Bar
Run by the Hotel Cipriani, this place, with tables by the canal looking across to Dorsoduro, has fantastic desserts (which is the main reason for stopping by). They also do full meals and snacks. Dress smartly.

☎ 041 522 48 44 ✉ Fondamenta San Biagio 773 ⏲ lunch & dinner Wed-Mon Apr-Oct ⚓ Palanca ♿

A place for snappy dressing; Harry's Dolci in Giudecca

CAFÉS & SWEETS

You could while away an afternoon indulging in an array of coffees (from espresso to Irish and beyond) in the elegance of what Napoleon once called 'Europe's finest drawing room', Piazza San Marco. Or maybe interrupt the sightseeing with a delicious gelato or pastry?

Alaska (Da Pistacchi) (3, C1) $
Gelateria
The *gelati* here have something of the mythical about them. The flavours are as real as the colours are vibrant. Opening times can be erratic; we have seen Alaska serving ice cream around midnight and shut in the morning.

☎ 041 71 52 11 ✉ Calle Larga dei Bari 1159 ⏲ 8am-1pm & 3-8pm ⚓ Riva de Biasio ♿

Bucintoro (3, E2) $
Pastry shop
Gino Zanin carries on antique Venetian traditions with his sweets and pastries, which come with such wonderful names as *bacingondola* (kiss in the gondola), which is a little meringue and chocolate number.

☎ 041 72 15 03 ✉ Calle del Scaleter 2229 ⏲ 7.15am-8pm Tue-Sun ⚓ San Stae

Mmm, gelato...

La passeggiata at Caffè Florian

Caffè Florian (3, H5) $$
Café
The plush interior of this, the city's best-known café, has seen the likes of Lord Byron and Henry James taking breakfast (separately) before they crossed the piazza to Caffè Quadri (see below) for lunch. Venetians started paying exorbitant sums for the pleasure of drinking here in 1720. In the warmer months a quartet plays for customers sitting outside (watch the surcharge on your drinks).
☎ 041 520 56 41
✉ Piazza San Marco, San Marco 56-59 ⏱ 9am-10pm Thu-Tue ⛴ Vallaresso & San Marco

Caffè Quadri (3, H4) $$
Café
Quadri is in much the same league as Florian, and equally steeped in history. Indeed, it actually opened its doors well before its better-known competitor, in 1683. It also has a restau-

rant and frequently presents a quartet of its own to compete with Florian in a good-natured fashion.
☎ 041 522 21 05
✉ Piazza San Marco, San Marco 120 ⏱ 9am-midnight Tue-Sun ⛴ Vallaresso & San Marco

Gelateria Nico (2, D5) $
Gelateria
Head here for some fine canalside ice cream. The locals take their evening stroll along the Zattere while eating their heavily laden cones. You can also just sit down for a juice or coffee.
☎ 041 522 52 93
✉ Fondamenta Zattere, Dorsoduro 922 ⏱ 6.45am-10pm Fri-Wed ⛴ Zattere ♿

Lavena (3, H4) $
Café
Founded in 1750 and a little less renowned than its big brothers (Florian

and Quadri), Lavena is in the same vein. Wagner was among its more visible customers, but historically gondoliers and *codegas* (stout fellows who lit the way home for people returning at night) also hung out here.
☎ 041 522 40 70
✉ Piazza San Marco, San Marco 133 ⏱ 9am-10pm Apr-Sep, 9am-10pm Wed-Mon Oct-Mar ⛴ Vallaresso & San Marco

Murano chandelier at Lavena

Entertainment

Venice, its inhabitants and its visitors constitute a theatrical spectacle in themselves. Good thing really because the lagoon city has long shed its 18th-century reputation as Europe's premier pleasure dome. The student population and steady stream of visitors keep a broad selection of enticing bars active, and there is an extraordinarily broad offering of theatre, opera and dance for such a small town. Do not, however, come to Venice for the clubbing! Things are busy until about 2am, beyond which it's slim pickings.

The reborn La Fenice theatre leads the way in the city's busy opera and performing-arts calendar, ably assisted by a handful of other theatres. Most drama is in Italian only. Other music options range from concerts of classical and baroque music to a little jazz or blues in a handful of venues.

There is really only one decent cinema in Venice itself and movies tend to be dubbed into Italian. Most locals gorge themselves on a year's worth of films at the annual September film festival.

Indeed, a string of festivals, traditional and arts, and above all the glorious Carnevale in February, fill the Venetian calendar throughout the year. The tourist offices can provide an updated list of events (p89).

For listings of bars, cafés, theatre and cinema, the best source is the monthly bilingual *VeNews* magazine, available at newsstands. *Un Ospite di Venezia*, a free monthly tourist information magazine, available (sometimes) at tourist offices and many hotels, contains less complete listings. You can also check out **Ombra.Net** (www.ombra.net).

Picking up Tickets

A national centralised ticket office with local outlets is **Box Office** (☎ 041 94 02 00; www.boxol.it), which has a few agents in Venice, including the travel agency **Gran Canal Viaggi** (3, G3; ☎ 041 271 21 11; Ponte dell'Ovo, San Marco 4759/4760). You can also book tickets with credit cards on the phone or online.

For some events, you can pick up tickets at **Vela** (☎ 041 24 24; www.velaspa.com) outlets, which are part of the ACTV city transport body. Vela operates kiosks in front of the train station and at Piazzale Roma.

Interactive art at the Biennale...

Special Events

January *Regatta delle Befane* – 6 January; the first of the year's more than 100 regattas, this features rowing Venetian-style (*voga veneta*), which involves various kinds of lagoon boats loosely resembling gondolas, whose crews row standing up

February *Carnevale* – Venetians don spectacular masks and costumes for this week-long party in the run-up to Ash Wednesday; starting dates for Carnevale in the next couple of years are 28 January 2005, 21 February 2006 and 13 February 2007 (see also p68)

April *Festa di San Marco* – 25 April; on the feast day of the city's patron saint, menfolk give their beloved a bunch of roses

May *Vogalonga* – some 3000 people and boats of all descriptions (powered by human muscle) participate in the 32km 'long row' from San Marco to Burano and back to the Grand Canal
Festa della Sensa – second Sunday in May; since AD 998 Venice has marked Ascension Day with the Sposalizio del Mar (Marriage to the Sea), a celebration of the city's profitable relationship with the sea (these days the mayor takes on the ducal role); this is celebrated with regattas off the Lido
Palio delle Quattro Antiche Repubbliche Marinare – late May to early June; Amalfi, Genoa, Pisa and Venice take turns to host the Historical Regatta of the Four Ancient Maritime Republics, in which four galleons compete; next in Venice in 2007

June *Marciliana* – medieval pageant in Chioggia to commemorate the siege of the city by Genoa in 1380; parades and competition between five *contrade* (town quarters) including rowing and archery
Sagra di San Pietro in Castello – last weekend in June; busy festival with music, drinking and eating at the steps of the church
Venezia Biennale Internazionale d'Arte – June to October/November; biennial international exhibition of visual arts held in permanent pavilions near the Giardini Pubblici and other locations throughout the city

July *Festa del Redentore* – third weekend in July; pontoon between Dorsoduro and Chiesa del SS Redentore on Giudecca is set up for thanksgiving celebrations for end of the plague in 1577; fireworks and regattas

September *Regatta Storica* – first Sunday in September; historic gondola race along the Grand Canal and parade of 15th century–style boats
Mostra del Cinema di Venezia – annual Venice International Film Festival, Italy's version of Cannes, held at the Palazzo del Cinema on the Lido

November *Festa della Madonna della Salute* – 21 November; procession on pontoon across the Grand Canal to the Chiesa di Santa Maria della Salute to give thanks for the city's deliverance from plague in 1630

BARS

The liveliest areas for bars are in and around the young and bustling Campo Santa Margherita in Dorsoduro (3, C4), along Fondamenta degli Ormesini (4, C2) and Fondamenta della Misericordia (4, D2–E2) in Cannaregio. More traditional wine bars, or *bacari*, generally close fairly early.

Ai Vini Padovani (3, C5)
An old-time *bacaro* where you can just settle at the red marble-topped bar for a wine and *cicheti*. Before WWII the bar used to get its wine from around Padua, which explains the name.
☎ 041 523 63 70
✉ **Calle dei Cerchieri 1280** ◷ 10am-10pm Mon-Fri 🚇 **Ca' Rezzonico**

It's never too early for a drink in Venice

Al Bottegon (Cantina di Vini già Schiavi; 3, D6)
Wander into this fusty old wine bar across from the Chiesa di San Trovaso for a glass of *prosecco* (see boxed text) beneath the bar's low-slung rafters and in the wavering light provided by dodgy bulbs. Locals have been doing just that for countless decades. Alternatively, you could buy a bottle of whatever takes your fancy and take it away.
☎ 041 523 00 34
✉ **Fondamenta Maravegie, Dorsoduro 992** ◷ 8am-9pm Mon-Sat 🚇 **Zattere**

Bacaro Lounge (3, G5)
You feel like you've been teletransported to New York or London in this cool downstairs cocktail lounge. You could head up the glass stairway to the restaurant above.
☎ 041 296 06 87 ✉ **Salizzada San Moisè, San Marco 1348** ◷ 10am-2am 🚇 **Vallaresso**

Bagolo (3, D2)
With its timber floors and low lighting inside, and candlelit tables outside, this spot lends a muted nocturnal buzz to this pretty square.
☎ 041 277 08 50
✉ **Campo San Giacomo dell'Orio, Santa Croce 1584** ◷ 7am-2am 🚇 **Riva de Biasio**

Café Noir (3, C4)
You can start the day with breakfast in here or hang out into the night with a mixed crowd of Italian students and foreigners. The place has a laid-back, underground feel about it.
☎ 041 71 09 25 ✉ **Calle San Pantalon, Dorsoduro 3805** ◷ 7am-2am Mon-Sat 🚇 **San Tomà**

Caffè (3, B4)
At the heart of the scene on Campo Santa Margherita is this perennially overcrowded student haunt. Known to

---

Make Mine Campari
In a country not noted for heavy drinkers, Venetians form a category all of their own. Locals can often be seen indulging in alcoholic cardiac stimulation at breakfast time and few skip the chance to have a *prosecco* (light sparking white wine) or two at some point in the day. Early evening is *aperitivo* time, and the favoured beverage is the *spritz* (*prosecco*, soda water and bitter — Campari, Amaro, Aperol or Select), one of the few things introduced by the Austrians in the 19th century that the Venetians actually appreciated. Later on, locals do not disdain a couple of classic Venetian cocktails, such as the Bellini (champagne or *prosecco* and peach nectar).

locals affectionately as the *caffè rosso* (the 'red café') because of the colour of the sign, it draws a happily hip crowd for snacks and drinks.
☎ 041 528 79 98
✉ Campo Santa Margherita, Dorsoduro 2693
🕓 7am-1am Mon-Sat
🚤 Ca' Rezzonico

Caffè Blue (3, C4)
Although it can get a little quiet on weekday evenings, this coolish student bar gets busy at weekends, especially when they put on a little live music. Even without, punters end up spilling out onto the street even in the big chill of winter.
☎ 041 523 72 27 ✉ Calle dei Preti, Dorsoduro 3778
🕓 8am-2pm & 5pm-2am Mon-Sat 🚤 San Tomà

Cavatappi (3, H4)
This modern creamy white bar with halogen lighting has wines from all over Italy and a metropolitan menu to match if you're feeling peckish.
☎ 041 296 02 52
✉ Campo della Guerra, San Marco 3805 🕓 9am-midnight Tue-Sat, 9am-8pm Sun 🚤 Vallaresso & San Marco

Centrale (3, G5)
In this modern restaurant is a comfortable lounge bar area for drinkers. The international, switched-on ambience throbs softly to chill-out and lounge sounds in this oddly 21st century–looking establishment.
☎ 041 296 06 64 ✉ Piscina Frezzeria, San Marco 1659/b 🕓 6.30pm-2am Mon-Sat 🚤 Vallaresso

Chet Bar (3, C4)
What a cheerful splash of modernity is this place with the black-and-white chessboard floor, plastic retro stools and bright lighting. It might sound like an odd mix but somehow it works in a city perhaps too used to classic décor.
☎ 041 523 87 27
✉ Calle de la Chiesa, Dorsoduro 3684 🕓 9am-1am Mon-Sat 🚤 Ca' Rezzonico

Harry's Bar (3, H5)
As well as being a noted restaurant, Harry's is, of course, first and foremost a bar. Everyone who is anyone and passing through Venice usually ends up here. Characters as diverse as Orson Welles and Truman Capote have sipped on a cocktail or two at Harry's.
☎ 041 528 57 77
✉ Calle Vallaresso, San Marco 1323 🕓 12-11pm
🚤 Vallaresso & San Marco

Imagina (3, C5)
Sit on fat white lounges around timber-topped tables over a wine or take a table on the street. The new management has had the bad taste to set up a softdrink machine inside, but it's still a pleasant place to hang.
☎ 041 241 06 25 ✉ Rio Terrà Canal, Dorsoduro 3126 🕓 8am-2am Mon-Sat 🚤 Ca' Rezzonico

Margaret Duchamp (3, C5)
Across the square from the above-mentioned Caffè (p63–4), the Margaret Duchamp is set at a strategic angle and perennially popular with a mixed crowd of locals, students and blow-ins. Perfect for seeing and being seen.
☎ 041 528 62 55
✉ Campo Santa Margherita, Dorsoduro 3019
🕓 9am-2am Wed-Mon
🚤 Ca' Rezzonico

Shaken, not Stirred
Truman Capote called a good Martini a Silver Bullet. What's in it? Quality gin and a drop of Martini Dry. Of course the amount of the latter varies according to taste: for a strong, dry Martini, 'rinse' the glass with Martini and then pour in freezing gin. Hemingway, who set part of his book *Across the River and into the Trees* at Harry's, had his own recipe: pour freezing cold gin into a glass dipped in ice, sit it next to a bottle of Martini for a moment, then drink!

Orange (3, C5)

The colour of an Aperol spritz, this hip locale appeals to a beautiful crowd that identifies with the fashion videos playing constantly. Skip the lurid bar and head out the back to the pleasant garden.

☎ 041 523 47 40
🖥 www.orangevenice
.com; ✉ Campo Santa
Margherita, Dorsoduro
3054/a 🕑 8am-2am
🚢 Ca' Rezzonico

Osteria agli Ormesini (4, C1)

Oodles of wine and 120 types of bottled beer in one knockabout little place? Perhaps you should get along to this *osteria*. It's something of a student haunt for those who like

that kind of gruff service and no-nonsense ambience.

☎ 041 71 38 34 ✉ Fondamenta degli Ormesini,
Cannaregio 2710
🕑 7am-2am Mon-Sat
🚢 Madonna dell'Orto

Taverna da Baffo (3, D2)

Named after Casanova's licentious poet pal Giorgio Baffo and lined with his rhymes in praise of 'the round arse' and other zones of the female anatomy, this bar has a young chirpy feel. In summer the tables outside are an especially pleasant spot to sip on a *spritz* or two.

☎ 041 520 88
62 ✉ Campiello
Sant'Agostin, Dorsoduro
2346 🕑 7am-2am Mon-
Sat 🚢 San Tomà

Vitae (Il Muro; 3, G4)

Il Muro (the wall) is busy by day with a lunchtime tippling crowd and again late on a Friday or Saturday night, when little else is happening in this part of town – it's a lively beacon of hedonism.

☎ 041 520 52 05
✉ Calle San Antonio, San
Marco 4118 🕑 7pm-2am
🚢 Vallaresso & San Marco

Racy rhymes of praise

CLUBS & CASINOS

Clubbing in Venice is poor. The Lido di Jesolo sees some action in summer – keep an eye on *VeNews* for details.

Casanova (4, A3)

A quick stumble from the train station, this is it, about the only place in Venice that can vaguely call itself a disco (more than it can a club). Each night has its own musical theme, from rock revival on Thursday to Latin on Friday and house on Saturday.

☎ 041 524 06 64
✉ Lista di Spagna, Cannaregio 158/a 🕑 11pm-
4am 🚢 Ferrovia

Casinò Municipale di Venezia (4, D3)

Housed in the Renaissance Palazzo Vendramin-Calergi, where the composer Richard

Wagner passed on in 1883, the gambler will find all his or her old favourites, from slot machines to roulette.

☎ 041 529 71 11
🖥 www.casinovenezia.it
✉ Palazzo Vendramin-
Calergi, Cannaregio 2040
€ €10 🕑 3.30pm-
2.30am 🚢 San Marcuola

Club Malvasia Vecchia (3, F5)

This social club functions as a late-night bar and dance den beloved of students and a hip artsy crowd; about the best option after 2am in all Venice.

☎ 041 522 58 83
✉ Corte Malatina,

San Marco 2586 € €15
one-off membership fee
🕑 11pm-4am Fri & Sat
🚢 Santa Maria del Giglio

Palazzo al Casinò

Magic Bus
Big and popular, Magic Bus administers a diet of anything from 90s rock to electronic sounds and occasionally stages live concerts.
☎ 041 595 21 15
🖥 www.magicbus.it
✉ Via delle Industrie 118, Marcon, Mestre
€ €8 🕒 11pm-5am Fri & Sat 🚇 Mestre, then taxi

Round Midnight (3, C5)
Not quite a club but more than a bar. This back-canal drink and dance den keeps punters from Campo Santa Margherita happy in the wee hours when all else closes. A mix of acid jazz, Latin and sometimes rockier sounds predominates. Opening times can be erratic – we have seen it in full swing in mid-July.
☎ 041 523 20 56
✉ Fondamenta dello

Squero, Dorsoduro 3102
€ €5 🕒 7pm-4am Mon-Sat Sep-May 🚤 Ca' Rezzonico

Zoobar
Another favourite in the Mestre area, this venue, out in Tessera, is virtually opposite Marco Polo airport.

In four dance spaces you can weave from house to Latin rhythms to mainstream international and Italian pop.
☎ 338-211 62 05
🖥 www.zoodisco.com
✉ Via Ca' Zorzi 2, Tessera
€ up to €20 🕒 9pm-4am Fri & Sat 🚌 5 & 55 or 🚤 to Mestre & taxi

Gay & Lesbian Venice
Virtually nothing is done to cater specifically for gays and lesbians in Venice, and the only thing for it is to head for a handful of places in Mestre and Padua. The big news is the gay sauna club in Mestre, **Metrò Venezia** (5, B1; ☎ 041 538 42 99; Via Cappuccina 82/b; €14; 🕒 2pm-2am), with several sauna and massage rooms, bar and dark room. In Padua half a dozen bars cater to the gay scene, including the **Flexo Video Bar** (☎ 049 807 47 07; www.flexoclub.it; Via Tommaseo 96a). There is also one gay club, **Black & White** (☎ 049 807 20 30; www.black-disco.com; Viale della Navigazione Interna 49b) in the industrial outskirts of town, along with a couple in satellite towns.

LIVE MUSIC, PERFORMING ARTS & CINEMA

Apart from those listed below, several smaller theatres are scattered about Venice, Mestre and the hinterland. Just as the grand opera theatre La Fenice has emerged from its scaffolding, the city's main drama stage, the Teatro Goldoni (3, G3), has been covered up for a makeover. If you are interested in baroque theatre, musical ensembles dressed in billowing 18th-century costume regularly perform concerts of baroque and light classical music from about Easter to the end of September. Clearly these shows are aimed at tourists and can be cheesy but the musical quality is not necessarily bad.

A handful of places – eateries and bars like Paradiso Perduto (p57) and Caffè Blue (p64) – intermittently put on live music, usually jazz, blues and mild pop. Watch the local press for annual events in Jesolo (1, E2) and Marghera (5, B1).

The cinema scene is limited in Venice and you will be unlikely to see anything in English. In July and August a big screen is erected in Campo San Polo, which makes for one of the more magical settings for outdoor cinema.

Al Vapore (5, B1)

About the best place for a consistent programme of jazz, blues and other music, Al Vapore is in Marghera, on the mainland. The club occasionally attracts good foreign acts as well as local talent.

☎ 041 93 07 96
🖥 www.alvapore.it
✉ Via Fratelli Bandiera 8, Marghera €) varies
🕙 7pm-2am Tue-Sun
🚉 to Mestre or 🚌 6, 6B, 66 & N2

Arsenale (2, G4)

Since the early 2000s La Biennale organisers have run several small theatre spaces in disused parts of the once mighty Venetian shipyards. They include the Teatro alle Tese, Corderie dell'Arsenale and Teatro Piccolo Arsenale.

🖥 www.labiennale.org
✉ Arsenale, Castello
🚊 Arsenale

Cinema Giorgione Movie d'Essai (3, H1)

The Giorgione is a comparatively modern cinema complex which presents a reasonable range of decent movies.

☎ 041 522 62 98 ✉ Rio Terrà Franceschi, Cannaregio 4612 🕙 2 or 3 sessions (around 4pm, 6pm & 9.15pm) 🚊 Fondamente Nuove 👶

Concerti della Venezia Musica

Divided into several different ensembles, such as the five-member Putte di Vivaldi (Vivaldi's Girls) and the grander I Virtuosi dell'Ensemble, this gang performs a range of Venetian baroque music, usually at the church where Vivaldi himself often worked, the Chiesa della Pietà (2, F5). In 2004 the concerts were temporarily transferred to **Palazzo Ca' Papafava** (4, F3; Calle della Racchetta, Cannaregio 3764).

☎ 041 520 87 67
🖥 www.vivaldi.it
✉ Chiesa della Pietà, Riva degli Schiavoni, Castello 4149 €) adult/student €25/15 🚊 San Zaccaria

Interpreti Veneziani

Since the mid-1980s this group has been presenting concerts of, above all, Venetian music in the Chiesa San Vidal (3, E5). Vivaldi, of course, heads the list but the musicians handle other Italian masters and the occasional interloper like Bach. They have performed as far afield as the Bayreuth festival and Melbourne, Australia.

☎ 041 277 05 61
🖥 www.interpreti veneziani.com ✉ Chiesa San Vidal, Campo San Vidal, San Marco 2862/b; €) adult/student €22/17; 🚊 Accademia

PalaFenice (2, A4)

This big-top theatre was created in 1996 to temporarily replace the Teatro La Fenice after fire largely destroyed the latter. Now that the grand old dame is back in action, this spot is still used for occasional concerts, theatre and other performances – in effect the city has gained another theatre.

☎ 041 78 65 75
🖥 www.teatrolafenice.it
✉ Tronchetto
🚊 Tronchetto

Teatro La Fenice (3, F5)

The grand opera theatre of Venice is back in action. This is an experience music lovers will not want to miss. The theatre has been restored to its former glory and equipped with the latest technology. First-night spots can cost several thousand euros. Some operas are staged at the 17th-century **Teatro Malibran** (3, H2; Calle del Teatro, San Marco 5870; €10-95) instead.

☎ 041 78 65 75
🖥 www.teatrolafenice .it ✉ Campo San Fantin, San Marco 1977 €) €20-1000 🚊 Santa Maria del Giglio

Teatro Malibran: grand opera in Venice

SPORT

Football

Tickets to see the local football side, **AC Venezia** (☎ 041 238 07 11; www
.veneziacalcio.it), play are available at the Stadio Penzo (2, H6) at the
eastern tip of the city and from Vela outlets such as those in front of
the train station (3, B1). They can cost around €15 to €20 depending on
the seat. Getting a ticket on the day is rarely a problem as this side generally muddles along in Serie B (second division).

Rowing & Sailing

Venetians love to get out on to the lagoon in one form of vessel or other.
Rowing and sailing regattas dot the city calendar and the keen can even
have a go themselves (see the boxed text on p34).

Rites of Spring

Venetians have been celebrating the approach of spring with Carnevale (Carnival)
since the 15th century. In those days private clubs organised masked balls, and
popular entertainment included bull-baiting and firing live dogs from cannons!
By the 18th century, Venice was home to hedonism and the licentious goings-on
of Carnevale lasted for two months.

Things quietened down after the city's fall to Napoleon in 1797. Revived in
1979, it has become the world's best-known baroque fancy dress party, as
extravagant as Rio's Carnival is riotous.

The festivities begin on a Friday afternoon (dates move around – see p62)
with a procession through the city. The official opening is on Saturday, when a
traditional masked procession leaves Piazza San Marco around 4pm and circulates
through the streets.

The following Thursday is Giovedì Grasso (Fat Thursday) and Friday afternoon's
highlight is the Gran Ballo delle Maschere (Grand Masked Ball) in Piazza San Marco.

Saturday and Sunday are given over to musical and theatrical performances in
Piazza San Marco. Also, on the Sunday, a procession of decorated boats and gondolas bearing masked passengers wends its way serenely down the Grand Canal.

The event winds up with a parade of the Re del Carnevale (Carnival King) and
the one-time guilds of the city.

The Kiss, Venetian style

Sleeping

Venice lives largely from tourism so it is no surprise that this compact city is jam-packed with hundreds of hotels and other digs. They range from simple family-run establishments to the extravagantly luxurious honey pots that draw celebs. The quality varies enormously and price does not always guarantee it. It is possible to find romantic rooms with ceiling frescoes in centuries-old *palazzi* (mansions) for much less than the often clinical rooms in some of the grander-sounding places.

Hotels around Piazza San Marco clearly feel obliged to charge extraordinary sums, especially when they look out over the Grand Canal or Bacino di San Marco. A bevy of budget hotels, convenient but frequently not great value, is cluttered around Rio Terrà Lista di Spagna (4, A3–B3), which leads from the train station towards the centre.

Increasingly, quality budget options, along with an array of mid-range and some grander places, are

Aim to stay in pointing distance of the Basilica di San Marco

spread further away from these standard poles of attention, in quieter corners of districts such as Dorsoduro, Santa Croce and Cannaregio. The occasional fine deal still lurks in the heart of San Marco and Castello.

Hotels go by other names too. The Italian *albergo* means hotel, while a *locanda* or *pensione* usually indicates a more modest family-run establishment.

Space is at a premium in Venice. Rooms are often small, even at pricey spots. In most upper-level hotels you can expect a standard array of amenities: phone, TV (often satellite), minibar, safe, air con, en suite bathroom with hairdryer, and 24-hour service. Only a few can offer extras such as pools. Mid-range places tend to offer only the phone, TV and air con. Rooms in cheaper locales often have only a washbasin, with a shared bathroom along the corridor.

Single travellers frequently get stung, as many hotels offer double rooms at only slightly reduced rates to loners.

Some hotels close in winter, especially those on the Lido, which can be shut from November to April. And finding a room on the Lido during the September cinema festival requires booking well in advance.

DELUXE

Bauer (3, G5)
If you don't mind the 1949 Soviet-style entrance, the canalside neo-Gothic frontage of this historic *palazzo* is sufficiently chic. The views across the Grand Canal are hard to beat. Elegant second-floor rooms drip Carrara marble and Murano glass.
☎ 041 520 70 22
🖥 www.bauervenezia.it
✉ Campo San Moisè, San Marco 1459 🚤 Vallaresso & San Marco 🍴 De Pisis

Cipriani (2, F6)
Set in the one-time villa of the Mocenigo noble family and surrounded by lavish grounds, the Cipriani has unbeatable views across to San Marco, and an elite feel. You can dine excellently in the hotel restaurant and a private launch runs between the hotel and San Marco.
☎ 041 520 77 44
🖥 www.hotelcipriani.it
✉ Giudecca 10 🚤 Zitelle 🍴 Cipriani Restaurant, Cip's Club, Terrace & Poolside Restaurants ♿

Old-style discreet service at the Gritti Palace

Luxury hotel Danieli: a feast for the eye

Danieli (3, J5)
Most of the rooms in this Venetian classic overlook the water. It opened as a hotel in 1822 in the 14th-century Palazzo Dandolo. Dining in the rooftop restaurant is a feast for the eyes as well as the palate.
☎ 041 522 64 80
🖥 www.starwood .com/luxury ✉ Riva degli Schiavoni, Castello 4196 🚤 San Zaccaria 🍴 La Terrazza & bars

Excelsior (5, E4)
A fanciful Moorish-style property, the Excelsior has long been the top address on the Lido. Many of the luxurious rooms look out to sea or across the lagoon to Venice. There are outdoor and heated pools if the beach seems too far away!
☎ 041 526 02 01
🖥 www.starwood .com/westin ✉ Lungomare Guglielmo Marconi 41, Lido 🚤 Lido 🍴 La Terrazza (summer only) & Tropicana ♿

Gritti Palace (3, F6)
Mix with celebs and royalty at one of the most famous hotels in Venice. A good portion of Hemingway's *Across the River and Into the Trees* is set in this 16th-century *palazzo*, loaded with marble, 18th-century furnishings and old-style discreet service.
☎ 041 79 46 11
🖥 www.starwood .com/luxury ✉ Campo Traghetto 2467 🚤 Santa Maria del Giglio 🍴 Club del Doge & Bar Longhi

San Clemente Palace (5, D3)
The rose-coloured buildings of the onetime monastery and madhouse of San Clemente make a unique setting. The hotel has 205 rooms and suites, two swimming pools, tennis courts, a golf course and wonderful gardens. The views out over the lagoon towards southern Venice and the Lido are truly romantic.
☎ 041 244 50 01
🖥 www.thi.it/english/ hotel/san_clemente ✉ Isola San Clemente 🚤 private shuttle from San Zaccaria 🍴 Ca' dei Frati, Le Maschere & La Laguna ♿

DAMIEN SIMONIS

TOP END

Ca' Pisani Hotel (3, D6)
Named after a 14th-century Venetian hero, this centuries-old building houses a self-conscious design–hotel, filled with 1930s and '40s furnishings and items especially made for the hotel. The rooms, some with exposed-beam ceilings, are full of pleasing decorative touches.
☎ 041 240 14 11
🖵 www.capisanihotel.it
✉ Rio Terrà Antonio Foscarini, Dorsoduro 979a
🚊 Accademia ✖ La Rivista

DD.724 (3, E6)
Take a centuries-old residence, pour in a wealth of modern design and contemporary art touches and you have Venice's second such hotel after Ca' Pisani (above). The seven rooms and suites are individually tailored, with features like LCD TV and home cinema. It looks on to the gardens of the Peggy Guggenheim Collection and a narrow *rio*.
☎ 041 277 02 62
🖵 www.dd724.it
✉ Dorsoduro 724 🚊 Accademia ✖ Ai Gondolieri (p53)

Hotel Ai Mori d'Oriente (4, D1)
One of the few luxury hotels in this part of the city, this charming two-storey, free-standing brick residence is just a stone's throw from the Ghetto. Richly coloured fabrics adorn all rooms, from the smallish standard doubles to the spacious suites. Try for a cosy attic room.
☎ 041 71 10 01
🖵 www.hotelaimori doriente.it ✉ Fonda-menta della Sensa, Cannaregio 3319 🚊 Orto ✖ Anice Stellato (p56)

Hotel Monaco & Grand Canal (3, G5)
This elegant 17th-century *palazzo* on the Grand Canal and a brisk stroll from Piazza San Marco is owned by the Benetton family and oozes an easy elegance. The rooms looking over the canal are the most sought after and the canalside terrace is magnificent. A major overhaul was completed in 2004.
☎ 041 520 02 11
🖵 www.summithotels .com ✉ San Marco 1325 🚊 San Marco & Valla-resso ✖ Terrace & Grand Canal Restaurant

Hotel San Cassiano (3, F1)
The 14th-century Ca' Favretto houses a selection of rooms: the best are high-ceilinged doubles overlook-ing the Grand Canal. The building is a wonderful old pile, with stone doorways along the staircases. Grab a table on the balcony for breakfast by the canal.
☎ 041 524 17 68
🖵 www.sancassiano.it
✉ Calle della Rosa, Santa Croce 2232 🚊 San Stae ✖ Vecio Fritolin (p55)

Locanda Cipriani (5, E1)
Feel like following in Papa's footsteps? You too can stay over for a night or two in one of the six spacious, tran-quil rooms at this country-lagoon getaway that found favour with Hemingway.
☎ 041 73 01 50
🖵 www.locanda cipriani.com ✉ Piazza Santa Fosca 29, Torcello 🚊 Torcello ✖ Locanda Cipriani ♿

Villa Mabapa (5, E3)
This pleasant hideaway, a grand old residence in a building dating from the 1930s with a couple of an-nexes offers spacious rooms with furniture ranging from the elegantly spare to art nouveau, depending on which you choose. Dine in the leafy garden.
☎ 041 526 05 90 or tollfree 800 277547
🖵 www.mabapa.it
✉ Riviera San Nicolò 16 🚊 Lido ✖ Ristorante Villa Mapaba ♿

The Bauer, dripping Carrara marble and Murano glass

MID-RANGE

Albergo Accademia Villa Maravege (3, D6)

Set in lovely gardens right by the Grand Canal and just a few steps away from the Gallerie dell'Accademia, this 17th-century villa has simple, elegant rooms, some with four-poster beds and timber floors. Most look on to the gardens and some have Canal glimpses.

☎ 041 521 01 88
🖥 www.pensione accademia.it ✉ Fondamenta Bollani, Dorsoduro 1058 🚊 Accademia

Albergo agli Alboretti (3, D6)

On arrival, you feel almost like you're stepping inside a cosy mountain chalet. Rooms are tastefully if simply arranged. They include three smallish suites. The restaurant, once frequented by Peggy Guggenheim and friends, is of a high standard.

☎ 041 523 00 58
🖥 www.aglialboretti .com ✉ Rio Terrà Antonio Foscarini, Dorsoduro 884 🚊 Accademia ✗ Ristorante agli Alboretti

La Calcina (2, D5)

John Ruskin wrote *The Stones of Venice* in this homely hotel, which has a smidgin of garden attached. The immaculate rooms are sober but charming with small terraces or views. Dine on the pontoon set on the canal.

☎ 041 520 64 66
🖥 www.lacalcina.com ✉ Fondamenta Zattere ai Gesuati, Dorsoduro 780 🚊 Zattere ✗ La Piscina

The homely and charming La Calcina

Locanda Antico Fiore (3, E4)

The front door of this 18th-century *palazzo* is on a narrow *rio* just in from the Grand Canal, so you could arrive in style by water taxi. Inside you will find cosy lodgings over a couple of floors. All rooms are tastefully decorated (tapestries, timber furniture), each with a different colour scheme.

☎ 041 522 7941
🖥 www.anticofiore .com ✉ Corte Lucatello, San Marco 3486 🚊 San Samuele ✗ Osteria al Bacareto (p52)

Locanda Art Deco (3, E5)

Bright, white-washed rooms with timber-beamed ceilings in this cheerful and immaculately kept hotel are especially enticing. Iron bedsteads are attached to comfy beds with orthopaedic mattresses – no chance of backache in Venice here!

☎ 041 277 05 58
🖥 www.locandaartdeco .com ✉ Calle delle Botteghe, San Marco 2966 🚊 Accademia ✗ Osteria al Bacareto (p52)

Locanda Leon Bianco (3, G2)

Up from an airless courtyard you chance upon this centuries-old jewel. The best three rooms (of eight) look right on to the Grand Canal. The undulating floors, heavy timber doors and original locks lend the rooms a timeless charm.

☎ 041 523 35 72
🖥 www.leonbianco.it ✉ Campiello Leon Bianco, Cannaregio 5629 🚊 Ca' d'Oro ✗ Osteria dalla Vedova (p57)

Antica Locanda Sturion (3, G3)

Two minutes from the Ponte di Rialto, this hotel has been taking in guests on and off since the 13th century. It has 11 rooms loaded with character. The best are the two generous ones overlooking the Grand Canal. The stairway up to the hotel seems endless.

☎ 041 523 62 43
🖥 www.locandasturion .com ✉ Calle del Sturion, San Polo 679 🚊 San Silvestro ✗ Trattoria alla Madonna

BUDGET

Antica Locanda Montin (3, C6)

Located on a quiet back canal a quick walk from the Gallerie dell'Accademia and the busy Campo Santa Margherita, it's been in business since the 1800s and the cosy rooms look either on to the canal or the rear garden. The rear pergola-covered dining area is enticing.

☎ 041 522 71 51
🖳 locandamontin@libero
.it ✉ Fondamenta di Borgo, Dorsoduro 1147
🚹 Accademia ✗ Antica Locanda Montin

Hotel Galleria (3, E6)

The Hotel Galleria is the only one-star hotel right on the Grand Canal, near the Ponte dell'Accademia. Space is a little tight, but the décor is welcoming. If you can get one of the rooms on the canal, how can you complain?

☎ 041 523 24 89
🖳 www.hotelgalleria.it
✉ Rio Terrà Antonio Foscarini, Dorsoduro 878/a
🚹 Accademia ✗ Ai Gondolieri (p53)

Hotel Galleria

Book Ahead

The **Associazione Veneziana Albergatori** (3, B1; ☎ 041 71 52 88; www.veneziasi.it; 🕑 8am-10pm Easter-Oct, 8am-9pm Nov-Easter) has offices at the train station, in Piazzale Roma and at the Tronchetto car park. Staff will book you a room but you must leave a small deposit and pay a minimal booking fee. It has 'last-minute' booking numbers: within Italy, freecall ☎ 800 84 30 06; from abroad ☎ 041 522 22 64.

Locanda Fiorita (3, E5)

Set on a wonderful square a spit away from the broad Campo Santo Stefano, the homey Locanda Fiorita offers simple, well-maintained rooms, some of which look on to the square. A few breakfast tables are set up outside.

☎ 041 523 47 54
🖳 www.locandafiorita
.com ✉ Campiello Nuovo, San Marco 3457/a
🚹 San Samuele ✗ Osteria al Bacareto (p52)

Pensione Guerrato (3, G2)

Amid the Rialto markets, this *pensione* is one of only two one-star places to have rooms with at least glimpses of the Grand Canal. It is housed in a former convent that (it is said) had served as a hostel for knights heading off on the Third Crusade.

☎ 041 528 59 27
🖳 web.tiscalinet.it/
pensioneguerrato
✉ Calle drio la Scimia, San Polo 240/a 🚹 Rialto
✗ Cantina Do Mori (p54)

Apartment Rental

An alternative to hotels is to rent an apartment. **Euroflats** (www.ccrsrl.com) has flats sleeping up to four from €700 per week. For luxury apartments try **Guest in Italy** (www.guestinitaly.com) or **Venetian Apartments** (www.venicerentals.com). You could pay €2000 per week sleeping up to six.

About Venice

HISTORY

A Swampy Refuge

Venice, it is claimed, was founded on a string of straggly malarial islets in the Venetian lagoon in AD 421. In 452 Attila the Hun and his marauding armies crashed into northeast Italy (aka the Veneto) and sent its inhabitants fleeing to the lagoon for safety. It was a pattern that would be repeated and in 726 (some sources say 697) the island communities came together under their first *doge* (duke). By the 9th century the administrative centre had become the islands around Rivo Alto (today Rialto). Over the succeeding centuries, by reclaiming land and creating artificial islands on beds of timber pylons, the Rivo Alto and its islands took on the present shape of Venice (Venezia) as it became known in the 12th century.

Venice Victorious

By 1095, when the First Crusade was called to liberate the Holy Lands from the Muslims, Venice had consolidated itself as an oligarchic republic under an elected *doge*.

Much of the city's power came from its ownership of territories in Dalmatia, Greece, the mainland and trading bases beyond. Venice ignored the sensibilities of other Christian powers and courted favours with whomever it pleased, including Muslim centres from Córdoba to Damascus.

The city's wily ambassadors attempted to keep sweet as many parties as possible, a game that led both Western European powers and Byzantium to be suspicious of the slippery lagoon city. Rival Italian sea powers, especially Genoa, were a constant source of competition, and in 1380 the Genoese attempted a siege of Venice only 30 years after the city had been decimated by the plague of 1348.

The Lion's Tale

Wherever Venice's law held sway, the Republic's ensign, the Lion of St Mark, fluttered. From the mists of medieval Venetian history, an elaborate tale emerged to explain how the lion came to represent Venice. An angel allegedly told the Evangelist St Mark (a lion in Christian iconography) that he would one day rest in the lagoon. In AD 828, in fulfilment of the prophecy, Venetian merchants smuggled his corpse out of Alexandria, Egypt. Hurrah! Now Venice could claim one of the big guns as its patron saint.

Through it all the Venetians continued to extend their power and by the time Constantinople fell to the Ottoman Turks in 1453, Venice had reached the height of its power. It ruled the Adriatic as a private lake, controlled strategic islands in Greece and held a mainland empire that stretched from Friuli in the east to Bergamo in the west.

Decline, Occupation & Unity

As the 15th century closed, the pressures on Venice grew. Turkey began to nibble away at the city's possessions and Venice could do little while the West remained disunited. Indeed, la Serenissima found itself on occasion fighting the Turks *and* Western powers.

The rounding of the Cape of Good Hope by the Portuguese at the end of the 15th century boded ill for Venetian trade, as did the rise of vigorous nation states like England and France. The fall of Crete to the Turks in the late 17th century was a further hammer blow.

Venice clung to its mainland possessions, but by the 18th century had lost its appetite for struggle. Venice came to be known throughout Europe as a party town, although its own noble class was increasingly destitute. Carnevale (see p68 for the modern version) lasted as long as two months, casinos did a roaring trade and Venetian prostitutes of every class were rarely short of clients.

The end of the Republic could not have been more ignominious. Napoleon marched into northern Italy in the late 1790s in pursuit of Austrian forces and swaggered into Piazza San Marco without firing a shot. The city subsequently ended up in Austrian hands until 1866, the year Venice joined the newly formed independent Kingdom of Italy.

The last decades of the 19th century saw trade pick up again. Industrial activity on Giudecca and the mainland got under way and the beginnings of tourism was an intimation of the city's future. Under Mussolini, the road bridge to the mainland was built.

Old black and white postcards of Venice

Venice Today

After WWII, industrial expansion on the mainland continued with the creation of a petrochemical complex that was good for the economy but noxious for the lagoon. In 1966 record floods devastated the city and it became apparent that it might one day be engulfed. People began to vote with their feet – the population today is less than half of what it was in the 1950s. Tourism, the annual film festival on the Lido and the arts and architecture Biennales keep Venice in the spotlight, but its long-term future as a functioning city seems uncertain.

ENVIRONMENT

Formed 6000 years ago by the meeting of the sea with freshwater streams running off Alpine rivers, the lagoon is like a shallow dish, crisscrossed by navigable channels (some natural, others of human construction). More than 40 islands dot the lagoon, the seaward side of which is protected by a 50km arc of long narrow islands (including the Lido) that stem the inward flow of the Adriatic.

From the 16th century, human intervention in maintaining the lagoon was stepped up with the diversion of freshwater streams away from the area around Venice to reduce sediment build-up. The 20th century brought more drastic changes. In the 1960s a deep channel was dug through to the petrochemical complex in Porto Marghera, which allows in supertankers and too much seawater.

Siren Call

Acqua alta (high water) officially begins at 0.8m above average sea level. Sixteen air-raid sirens around the city go off if it is expected to hit 1.1m. Over 1.2m you can be in trouble, as even the walkways set up in strategic parts of town are no use, and at 1.4m a state of emergency is declared. The November 1966 flood level was 1.94m.

San Marco and Castello from San Giorgio Maggiore

DAMIEN SIMONIS

Flooding in Venice has always been a problem. In winter, high Adriatic tides push into the lagoon and inundate the city. The record 1966 floods set alarm bells ringing and in 2003 work began on the controversial Mose project to fit the lagoon's sea entrances with mobile barriers. If all goes well, they could be in place by 2012. A

> **Did You Know?**
> - Population 64,000 (Venice proper); 270,000 (total municipality)
> - Inflation rate 2.8%
> - GDP per capita €23,500 (Veneto region)
> - Unemployment 4.6% (Venice province)

combination of subsidence (at least 14cm in the 20th century) and rising average sea levels (9cm) means that the city is literally sinking!

GOVERNMENT & POLITICS

Venice is the capital of the Veneto region (one of 20 in Italy), which extends west to Verona and Lake Garda, and north into the Alps. The Veneto region is subdivided into seven provinces, of which the area around Venice – Venezia – is one.

Since 1927, the *comune*, or municipality, of Venice has comprised the islands of the lagoon (including Murano, Burano, Torcello, the Lido and Pellestrina), as well as Mestre, Porto Marghera and Chioggia and other centres on the mainland. Locals divide the lot into three areas: *terraferma* (mainland), *centro storico* (Venice proper, including Giudecca) and the *estuario* (remaining islands). Venice is made up of six *sestieri* (neighbourhoods).

Since 2000 the mayor of Venice has been Paolo Costa, who heads a left-of-centre coalition, often at loggerheads with the Veneto region's government, run by the right-wing Prime Minister Silvio Berlusconi's Forza Italia party. All three levels of government buried their differences to get the long-delayed Mose lagoon barrier project into motion in 2002–3.

The game of power continues to play itself out in Venice

ECONOMY

The mainstays of Venice's economy are tourism and the mainland petro-chemical industry in Porto Marghera. The Veneto region, long a rural back-water, took off economically in the 1970s and 1980s, largely due to small industries and family businesses (such as Treviso-based Benetton). The Veneto contains almost 8% of Italy's population and contributes about 12% of exports.

Tourism is pivotal in Venice. In 2002 the city hall estimated 2.7 million visitors (down on earlier years) stayed at least one night in the lagoon city. Anything from 15 million to 20 million day-trippers (people who don't stay overnight and leave no statistical trace) pour in annually. The downturn in overnight stays combined with a boom in recent years in hotel openings means that visitors can more often squeeze a better price out of hoteliers. The latter are not desperate, but can no longer count on full houses.

Of the lagoon's remaining traditional industries, principally boat-building and fishing, glass-making is the one with the most prominent profile. Although clearly directed at the tourist trade, some of the work coming out of Murano's glass factories is of the highest quality.

SOCIETY & CULTURE

With so many tourists wandering around, finding a full-blooded Venetian can be a tall order! Some of the great aristocratic names survive and their families often retain enormous lodgings in the city's grander palaces. Small pockets of more working-class Venetians and fishing families also continue to live in the city, shoulder to shoulder with a big student popu-lation made up of locals and people from all over the country.

An island city, it has something of a village feel – there is no car culture and people are obliged to walk around or use public transport; locals frequently run into friends or acquaintances, stop for a chat or a quick drink and then head on their way. Locals seem to have developed a mechanism that allows the floods of visitors to be invisible to them.

Venetians love a sociable tip-ple in the city's many bars and squares. In summer, some zip off on their speedboats to spend the day on little lagoon beaches on Sant'Erasmo or catch the ferry to the Lido for the seaside. The win-ter chic crowds head off to ski in Cortina in the Alps.

Although the majority of Vene-tians profess to be Catholics, many do not practise.

Fruit stall holder on Sottomarina Beach

ARTS
Architecture

Apart from a few Roman vestiges found on Torcello and the mainland, the earliest reminders we have of building in the lagoon are the 7th- and 9th-century apses of the **Cattedrale di Santa Maria Assunta** (p19) on Torcello. The church is a mix of Byzantine and Romanesque. The latter style developed in the West and is characterised by use of the semicircle for arches, apses and so on. Byzantine influences are clearest in the use of decorative mosaics.

By far the grandest example of style mixing is the **Basilica di San Marco** (pp8–9). It is a grand Byzantine work, with touches ranging from Romanesque to Renaissance.

Venice put its own spin on Gothic. The two grand churches of the Franciscan and Dominican orders, the **Frari** (p14) and **SS Giovanni e Paolo** (p23), are towering, austere creations built in brick and eschewing external decoration. The white-and-pink marble **Palazzo Ducale** (p10) is the most stunning example of late-Gothic secular construction.

The Renaissance brought a return to the study of classical lines, clear in Andrea Palladio's (1508–80) **Chiesa di San Giorgio Maggiore** (p21) and **Chiesa del SS Redentore** (p31). Jacopo Sansovino (1486–1570) was another key Renaissance architect. The baroque architect Baldassare Longhena (1598–1682) dominated the 17th century, just as his **Chiesa di Santa Maria della Salute** (p22) presides over the south end of the Grand Canal.

> ### Dos & Don'ts
> Dress with decorum in Venice's churches. This means no shorts and no short skirts. Shoulders must be covered. These rules are enforced rigorously at the Basilica di San Marco and some other churches.

The busy façade of the Basilica di San Marco

Painting

The glory days of Venetian art came with the Renaissance, starting with the **Bellini** family, especially Giovanni. He was followed by **Vittore Carpaccio** (1460–1526), **Cima da Conegliano** (c1459–c1517), **Giorgione** (1477–1510) and **Lorenzo Lotto** (c1480–1556). They laid the foundations for what was to come, a star burst of greatness that thrust Venice into the forefront of European painting.

A Canaletto style image on a gondola in the Grand Canal

When his *Assunta* was unveiled in the Frari church (p14), **Titian** (c1490–1576) was revealed as an unparalleled genius of the late Renaissance. He only just overshadowed **Tintoretto** (1518–94), best known for his paintings that fill the Scuola Grande di San Rocco (p14), and **Paolo Veronese** (1528–88), who had a hand in the decoration of the Doge's Palace (p10). A lesser host of artists producing fine works beavered away in the shadow of these greats.

Giambattista Tiepolo (1696–1770) was the uncontested king of Venetian rococo, followed by his son **Giandomenico** (1727–1804). At about the same time the *vedutisti* (landscape painters) were also at work. The photo-sharp images of Venice by **Canaletto** (1697–1768) are known the world over.

Sculpture

Fine Romanesque sculpture adorns the Basilica di San Marco, and some of the *doges'* tombs in the Chiesa di SS Giovanni e Paolo are worthy Gothic-era contributions.

Antonio Canova (1757–1822), born in Possagno, spent his early years in Venice but ended up in Rome as the country's most celebrated sculptor. A few of his works can be seen in the **Museo Correr** (p24).

Chiesa della Pietà: Vivaldi's church

Music

The greatest name to come out of Venice was **Antonio Vivaldi** (1678–1741), born in Castello. He left a vast repertoire behind him, of which the best concerto is *Le Quattro Stagioni* (The Four Seasons). You can visit his church, Chiesa della Pietà. **Tomaso Albinoni** (1671–1750) produced some exquisite music, including the sublime *Adagio in G Minor*.

Directory

DAMIEN SIMONIS

ARRIVAL & DEPARTURE

Air

Most flights arrive at Marco Polo Airport (1, D2), 12km from the city on the mainland. Others arrive at Treviso's San Giuseppe Airport (1, D1), 30km north of Venice.

MARCO POLO AIRPORT
Information
General Enquiries &
Flight Information   ☎ 041 260 92 60

Airport Access
Bus Services run to Piazzale Roma (2, C4) via Mestre station. **ATVO Fly Bus** (☎ 041 520 55 30; www.atvo.it; €3). The service runs from 8.30am to 12.30am. **Azienda Consorzio Trasporti Veneziano** (ACTV; ☎ 041 528 78 86; €1.50) city bus No 5 also serves the airport.

Boat Fast ferry from the airport costs €10 to Venice (1¼ hours) or the Lido (one hour) and €5 to Murano (30 minutes). Pick it up at the Zattere (2, D5) or in front of the Giardini ex-Reali (3, H6). **Alilaguna** (☎ 041 522 19 39; www.alilaguna.it).

Water Taxi The rate for the ride between the airport and Piazzetta di San Marco (30 minutes) is about €80 for four people.

Taxi More prosaic are land taxis, €25 to €30 from the airport to Piazzale Roma (15 minutes).

SAN GIUSEPPE AIRPORT
Information
General Enquiries &
Flight Information   ☎ 0422 31 53 31

Airport Access
Bus The **Eurobus** (☎ 041 541 51 80) service runs to/from Piazzale Roma (one way/return €4.50/8).

Train Local bus No 6 goes to the main train station in Treviso. From there you can proceed to Venice by rail.

Bus

Although it is possible to reach Venice by bus from some other cities in Italy, it is generally preferable to travel by rail. The main trans-European bus company, **Eurolines** (www.eurolines.com), is represented by **Agenzia Brusutti** (3, A2; ☎ 041 520 55 30; Piazzale Roma 497/e).

Train

Trenitalia (☎ 892021; www.tren italia.it) operates services from most major Italian cities. International trains run to Venice from Geneva, Munich and Vienna. Otherwise you'll need to change trains.

Trains stop in Venice at Stazione di Santa Lucia (2, C3) and at Mestre (5, B1), on the mainland.

From London you can get the **Orient Express** (☎ 0845-077 2222 in the UK; www.orient-express .com) for a special way to travel to Venice.

Boat

Ferries run year round from Greece to Venice. In Venice you can contact **Minoan Lines** (www .minoan.gr), which is at the passenger port (Stazione Marittima; 2, C5).

Travel Documents
PASSPORT
You need a valid passport (or ID card for EU, Norwegian and Swiss citizens) to enter Italy.

VISA
Nationals of Australia, Canada, Israel, Japan, New Zealand and the USA don't need a visa if entering as tourists for up to 90 days. Others and those wishing to stay for longer periods should check with their nearest Italian consulate.

Customs & Duty Free
There are no limits on the importation of euros. People entering Italy from outside the EU are allowed to bring in duty-free up to one bottle of spirits, one bottle of wine, 50mL of perfume and 200 cigarettes. People travelling within the EU are allowed to import VAT-free goods (on sale at European airports).

Left Luggage
The *deposito* (left luggage) at Marco Polo airport is in the arrivals hall and is open 5.30am to 9pm. There is no such facility at San Giuseppe airport.

GETTING AROUND
Walking is the best way to get to know the city, but there are plenty of other options. The **ACTV** (www .actv.it) runs the *vaporetto* (water bus) network in Venice and buses to Mestre and other mainland areas. Water taxis are the other option. Wheeled taxis run from Piazzale Roma to the mainland. For information you can call **Vela** (☎ 041 24 24; www.velaspa.com).

Travel Passes
Those planning to use the *vaporetti* even moderately are advised to buy a *biglietto a tempo*, a ticket that is valid on all transport (except the Alilaguna, Clodia, Fusina and LineaBlù services). Valid for 24 hours from the first validation, they cost €10.50. *Biglietto tre giorni*, a three-day version, costs €22 (€15 with a Rolling Venice pass; see p85). Buy passes at ACTV and Vela outlets and some *tabacchi* (tobacconists) and *edicole* (newsstands).

The **Venice Card** (☎ 041 24 24; www.venicecard.it) is another option. The blue card gives unlimited use of ferries and buses throughout Venice for one, three or seven days, and free access to public toilets (otherwise €0.50). The orange version throws in a series of sights, the most important of which is the Palazzo Ducale.

The junior (under 29) cards cost €9/22/49 for one/three/seven days, while the senior versions cost €14/29/51. The junior orange cards cost €18/35/61 and the senior version €28/47/68.

Vaporetto
Several *vaporetto* lines run up and down the Grand Canal, although some are *limitato* (limited-stops services). You can be sure that all will stop at St Mark's, Accademia, Rialto, Ferrovia (for the train station) and Piazzale Roma. Line No 1 is an all-stops job that takes a little over 30 minutes to meander between Ferrovia and St Mark's.

Tickets must be bought in advance and validated prior to boarding. Single-trip tickets cost €3.50

(return €6) – so travel passes make good sense. Timetables are listed at stops. Some lines start as early as 5.30am and others stop operating by as early as 9pm. A night (N) service runs along the Grand Canal and serves the Lido and Giudecca. Similar services also serve the main lagoon islands. None operate beyond about 4.30am.

Traghetto

The *traghetto* is a commuter gondola that crosses the Grand Canal at strategic spots and saves on a lot of shoe leather. Some operate from about 9am to 6pm, while others stop at around midday. A crossing costs €0.40 and passengers stand.

Water Taxi

Water taxis (☎ 041 240 67 11) are prohibitively expensive, with a flagfall of €8.70 and €1.30 for every minute of travel, an extra €6 if you order one by telephone, and various surcharges that make a gondola ride seem affordable. Rogue water taxi operators work the Tronchetto area and insist there are no *vaporetti* from there. Ignore them and head for the *vaporetto* stop. A typical trip across Venice will cost around €50 for up to four passengers.

Bus

Regular buses (including a night service) run from Piazzale Roma to Mestre (from outside the train station) and other mainland destinations. Tickets cost €1 (or €9 for 10 rides) and must be bought at newsstands or tobacconists prior to boarding.

Train

All trains leaving Stazione di Santa Lucia stop in Mestre. Tickets (available from newsstands at the train station) cost €1 on the regular, slower trains. The last trains run around midnight – check timetables posted at either train station.

Taxi

You can call a **taxi** (☎ 041 93 62 22) for trips to Mestre or the airport starting from Piazzale Roma, or just turn up at the taxi ranks.

Car & Motorcycle

You cannot drive anywhere in Venice, except off to the mainland from the car parks around Piazzale Roma and Tronchetto.

PRACTICALITIES
Business Hours

Public offices tend to open from 8.30am to about 2pm Monday to Friday. Regular business hours are from 8.30am to 1.30pm and from 4pm to 7.30pm Monday to Friday. A few larger stores tend to open through lunch. Many stores open on Saturday and some directed mainly at tourists open on Sunday, too.

Banks are generally open from 8.30am to 1.30pm and from 3.30pm to 4.30pm Monday to Friday. Some main branches are also open from 9am to 12.30pm on Saturday. Hours have a tendancy to vary a little from bank to bank. The Bureaux de change tend to open from 8am to 8pm, Monday to Saturday.

Climate & When to Go

It's almost always high season in Venice, although the city is busiest in spring (Easter to June) and early autumn (September to October). Accommodation can also be hard to find around Christmas and New Year, and Carnevale (February). July and August tend to be oppressively hot and humid, while winters can be grey and wet, with flooding a frequent occurrence in November and December. Venice is at its best in early spring, but some find the mists of early winter (if and when they strike) enchanting.

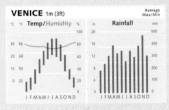

Disabled Travellers

Venice is not a dream location for the disabled, but it is not impossibly difficult. The map from Azienda di Promozione Turistica (APT) offices (p89) has areas of the city shaded in yellow, indicating that they can be negotiated without running into a bridge. Some bridges are equipped with lifts (montascale) that are marked on the maps. You can get hold of a key to operate these lifts from the tourist offices. Some vaporetto lines allow wheelchair access. You can get two wheelchairs on the lines 1 and 82 boats at a time. Six buslines are adapted for wheelchair users, including No 2 (Piazzale Roma–Mestre train station) and those for the airport.

Slight modifications have been made to some of the city's sights to facilitate access to those in wheelchairs.

INFORMATION & ORGANISATIONS

In Venice try **Informahandicap** (☎ 041 534 17 00; informa handicap@comune.venezia.it; Villa Franchin, Via Garibaldi 155, Mestre) for local information. It has a branch in the town hall building of **Ca' Farsetti** (3, F3 ☎ 041 274 80 80; San Marco 4136). Worth checking out is **Accessible Travel & Leisure** (☎ 01452-729739; www .accessibletravel.co.uk; Avionics House, Naas Lane, Gloucester GL2 4SN). It claims to be the biggest UK travel agent dealing with travel for the disabled.

Discounts

Admission to state museums (there are just three in Venice) is free for EU citizens under 18 and over 65. Otherwise there are precious few reductions for sights and none (except for students resident in Venice) for public transport.

STUDENT & YOUTH CARDS

International student cards don't open many doors in Venice. Those aged 14 to 29 can obtain a **Rolling Venice card** (€3) at tourist offices and Vela outlets (3, B1).

Electricity

Voltage	220V
Frequency	50Hz
Cycle	AC
Plugs	standard continental two round pins

Embassies & Consulates

Most countries have embassies in Rome and a few are represented by consulates in Venice. Where there is no representation in Venice, the nearest available embassy or consulate is listed:

Australia (☎ 02 77 70 41; Via Borgogna 2, Milan)

Canada (☎ 049 876 48 33; Riviera Ruzzante 25, Padua)

New Zealand (☎ 06 441 71 71; Via Zara 28, Rome)

UK (5, B1; ☎ 041 505 59 90; Piazzale Donatori di Sangue 2, Mestre)

USA (☎ 02 29 03 51; Largo Donegani 1, Milan)

Emergencies

Ambulance	☎ 118
Carabinieri (military police)	☎ 112
Fire	☎ 115
Police	☎ 113
Rape Crisis Line	☎ 041 269 06 10

Fitness

A couple of small municipal swimming pools operate (except in summer), with complex timetables (contact them for details) along with a handful of small gyms.

GYMS & HEALTH CLUBS

Palestra Body World (3, E1; ☎ 041 71 56 36; Calle del Ravano, Santa Croce 2196/a; €10 valid 60 days €65; 🕑 9am-10pm Mon-Fri, 9am-1pm Sat Sep-May, 9am-10pm Mon-Fri Jun-Aug; 🚊 San Stae)

Palestra Club Delfino (2, D5; ☎ 041 523 27 63; www.palestraclubdelfino .com; Fondamenta Zattere, Dorsoduro 788/a; €13; 🕑 9am-10pm Mon-Fri, 9am-noon Sat; 🚊 Zattere)

SWIMMING POOLS

Piscina Comunale a Chimisso (2, B6; ☎ 041 528 54 30; Sacca S Biagio, Giudecca; €4.50; 🕑 Sep-Jun; 🚊 Sacca Fisola)

Piscina Comunale di Sant'Alvise (2, D2; ☎ 041 71 35 67; Campo Sant'Alvise, Cannaregio 3161; €4.50; 🕑 mid-Sep–mid-Jul; 🚊 Sant'Alvise)

Gay & Lesbian Travellers

Homosexuality is legal in Italy and well tolerated in Venice and the north in general. The legal age of consent is 16. However, overt displays of affection by homosexual couples could attract a negative response. In Venice there's little in the way of a gay scene, with no overtly gay establishments.

Health
PRECAUTIONS

Venice's tap water is safe to drink (although many people prefer the bottled stuff) and food preparation is generally hygienic. Heat and humidity might be a problem in summer – wear a hat and loose, comfortable clothing and drink plenty of fluids.

MEDICAL SERVICES

Hospitals with 24-hour emergency departments include:

Ospedale Civile (3, J2; ☎ 041 529 41 11 or 041 529 45 17; Campo SS Giovanni e Paolo, Castello 5666)

Ospedale Umberto I (5, B1; ☎ 041 260 71 11; Via Circonvallazione 50, Mestre)

DENTAL SERVICES

You can get urgent dental treatment at the Ospedale Civile (see p86).

PHARMACIES

Pharmacies (*farmacie*) are usually open from 9am to 12.30pm and from 3.30pm to 7.30pm. Most close on Saturday afternoon and Sunday. Information on all-night pharmacies is listed in *Un Ospite di Venezia*, a free booklet available at tourist offices and some hotels.

Holidays

1 Jan	New Year's Day
6 Jan	Epiphany
Mar/Apr	Good Friday
Mar/Apr	Easter Monday
25 Apr	Liberation Day
1 May	Labour Day
15 Aug	Feast of the Assumption
1 Nov	All Saints' Day
8 Dec	Feast of the Immaculate Conception
25 Dec	Christmas Day
26 Dec	Boxing Day

Internet
INTERNET CAFÉS

Net House (3, E5; ☎ 041 520 81 28; Campo Santo Stefano 2958-2967, San Marco; per hr €7; ✆ 8am-3am)

Venice Internet Point (4, A3; ☎ 041 275 82 17; Rio Terrà Lista di Spagna, Cannaregio 149; per hr €8; ✆ 9am-midnight)

USEFUL WEBSITES

The **Lonely Planet website** (www.lonelyplanet.com) has links to many Venetian websites. Others to try include:

ENIT (Italian State Tourist Board) www.enit.it
Ombra.Net www.ombra.net
Comune di Venezia www.comune.venezia.it

Lost Property

For items lost on *vaporetti* call ☎ 041 272 21 79, or on the train ☎ 041 78 52 38. Otherwise, call the local police (*vigili urbani*) on ☎ 041 522 45 76. The lost property office is at Piazzale Roma (3, A2).

Metric System

The metric system is standard and, like other continental Europeans, Italians use commas in decimals and points to indicate thousands.

TEMPERATURE
$°C = (°F - 32) ÷ 1.8$
$°F = (°C \times 1.8) + 32$

DISTANCE
1in = 2.54cm
1cm = 0.39in
1m = 3.3ft = 1.1yd
1ft = 0.3m
1km = 0.62 miles
1 mile = 1.6km

WEIGHT
1kg = 2.2lb
1lb = 0.45kg
1g = 0.04oz
1oz = 28g

VOLUME
1L = 0.26 US gallons
1 US gallon = 3.8L
1L = 0.22 imperial gallons
1 imperial gallon = 4.55L

Money
ATMS

Automatic Teller Machines (ATMs) are in busy squares and streets, especially in areas between Lista di Spagna, Strada Nova and the train station; also try around the Rialto and Piazza di San Marco.

CREDIT CARDS

Visa and MasterCard are the most widely accepted cards in Italy. Small hotels and restaurants sometimes don't accept cards. For 24-hour card cancellations or assistance, call:

AmEx	☎ 800 87 43 33
Diners Club	☎ 800 86 40 64
MasterCard	☎ 800 87 08 66
Visa	☎ 800 81 90 14

CURRENCY

Italy's currency is the euro. There are seven euro notes in denominations of €500, €200, €100, €50, €20, €10 and €5. The eight euro coins come in denominations of €2 and €1, then 50, 20, 10, five, two and one cents.

MONEYCHANGERS

It is thought that banks generally offer the fairest rates and lowest commissions. The latter can vary from a fixed fee of €1.50 to a percentage. The post office is also worth checking out. Bureaux de change commissions can be hefty (as high as 10%!).

TRAVELLERS CHEQUES

Travellers cheques can be cashed at any bank or exchange office (watch commissions).
American Express (3, G5; ☎ 041 520 08 44; Salizzada San Moisè, San Marco 1471; ☺ 9am-5.30pm Mon-Fri, 9am-12.30pm Sat)
Travelex (3, H4; ☎ 041 528 73 58; Piazza San Marco 142; ☺ 8.45am-8pm Mon-Sat, 9am-6pm Sun) Has branch at Riva del Ferro 5126 (3, G3).

Newspapers & Magazines

Major Italian dailies include *Corriere della Sera* and *La Repubblica*. The local dailies are *Il Gazzettino* and *Nuova Venezia*. A handy local publication is *VeNews*, a monthly magazine in Italian and English.

Post

The main post office (3, G3; ☎ 160; www.poste.it; Salizzada del Fondaco dei Tedeschi; ☺ 8.30am-6.30pm Mon-Sat) is just near the Ponte di Rialto. You can buy stamps here or from tobacconists (look for the *tabacchi* sign).

POSTAL RATES

Postcards and letters up to 20g sent priority post *(posta prioritaria)* cost €1 to Australia and New Zealand, €0.80 to the Americas, €0.62 within Europe and to Mediterranean countries, and €0.60 within Italy.

Radio

There are three state-owned stations: RAI-1 (1332AM or 89.7FM), RAI-2 (846AM or 91.7FM) and RAI-3 (93.7FM). Radio Venezia (101.1FM) has news and a reasonable selection of music.

Telephone

A local call on a public phone costs about €0.25 for three minutes. Orange Telecom Italia phone booths are spread across the city.

PHONECARDS

Telecom Italia phonecards (€2.50 or €5) are available from post offices, tobacconists and some newsstands.

Some Internet centres provide cut-rate international call facilities.

MOBILE PHONES

Italy uses the GSM cellular phone system, compatible with phones sold in the rest of Europe, Australia and most of Asia, but not those from North America and Japan (unless you have a tri-band handset).

COUNTRY & CITY CODES

The city code (including the 0) is an integral part of the number and must be dialled, whether calling from next door or abroad; mobile numbers have no initial 0. The codes are:

Italy	☎ 39
Venice	☎ 041

USEFUL PHONE NUMBERS

Local Directory Enquiries	☎ 12
International Directory Enquiries	☎ 176
International Operator	☎ 170
Reverse-Charge (collect)	☎ 170
Reverse-Charge Europe	☎ 15
International Access Code	☎ 00

Television

The three state-run stations, RAI-1, RAI-2 and RAI-3, compete with the private Canale 5, Italia 1, Rete 4 and La 7 stations, to provide a diet of talk and variety shows and the occasional decent programme (especially on RAI-3). A growing number of hotels have BBC World, CNN, Sky Channel and others.

Time

Venice Standard Time is one hour ahead of GMT/UTC. Daylight savings is practised from the last Sunday in March to the last Sunday in October.

Tipping

In restaurants where service is not included it's customary to leave a 10% tip. In bars, Italians often leave small change. You should tip the porter at upmarket hotels (about €0.50/bag).

Toilets

Public toilets (visitors pay €0.50, residents €0.25) are scattered about Venice – look for the 'WC Toilette' signs. Hours vary (7am-7pm or 9am-8pm).

Tourist Information

In Venice there is one **central information line** (☎ 041 529 87 11; www.turismovenezia.it).

The main APT office is at **Piazza San Marco** (3, H5; Piazza San Marco 71/f; ☽ 9am-3.30pm Mon-Sat). Others are in the **Venice Pavilion** (3, H5; ☽ 10am-6pm), **train station** (3, B1; ☽ 8am-6.30pm), **Piazzale Roma** (2, C4; Garage Comunale; ☽ 9.30am-6.30pm) and the arrivals hall of **Marco Polo airport** (5, D1; ☽ 9.30am-7.30pm).

Women Travellers

Of the main destinations in Italy, Venice has to be the safest for women. If you do get unwanted attention, whatever methods you use to deal with it at home should work here.

Tampons (and more commonly sanitary towels) are available in pharmacies and supermarkets. Prescriptions are needed for the contraceptive pill.

LANGUAGE

True-blue Venetians speak a dialect (for some a separate language), known commonly as Venessian. Here are some useful phrases to get you started. Grab a copy of Lonely Planet's *Italian Phrasebook* if you'd like to know more.

Basics

Hello.	*Buongiorno.* (pol)
	Ciao. (inf)
Goodbye.	*Arrivederci.* (pol)
	Ciao. (inf)
Yes.	*Sì.*
No.	*No.*
Please.	*Per favore/*
	Per piacere.
Thank you.	*Grazie.*
You're welcome.	*Prego.*
Excuse me.	*Mi scusi.*
Do you speak English?	*Parla inglese?*
I don't understand.	*Non capisco.*
How much is it?	*Quanto costa?*

Getting Around

When does the ... leave/arrive?	*A che ora parte/arriva ...?*
bus	*l'autobus*
boat	*la barca*
train	*il treno*
I'd like a ...	*Vorrei un*
ticket	*biglietto di ...*
one-way	*solo andata*
return	*andata e ritorno*
Where is ...?	*Dov'è ...?*

Accommodation

Do you have any rooms available?	*Avete delle camere libere?*
a ... room	*una camera ...*
single	*singola*
twin	*doppia*
double	*matrimoniale*

Around Town

I'm looking for ...	*Cerco ...*
the market	*il mercato*
a public toilet	*un gabinetto*
What time does it open/close?	*A che ora (si) apre/chiude?*

Eating

breakfast	*prima colazione*
lunch	*pranzo*
dinner	*cena*
The bill, please.	*Il conto, per favore.*

Time, Days & Numbers

What time is it?	*Che ora è?*
Monday	*lunedì*
Tuesday	*martedì*
Wednesday	*mercoledì*
Thursday	*giovedì*
Friday	*venerdì*
Saturday	*sabato*
Sunday	*domenica*
1	*uno*
2	*due*
3	*tre*
4	*quattro*
5	*cinque*
6	*sei*
7	*sette*
8	*otto*
9	*nove*
10	*dieci*
100	*cento*
1000	*mille*

Index

See also separate indexes for Eating (p94), Sleeping (p94), Shopping (p94) and Sights with map references (p95).

EATING

SLEEPING

SHOPPING

Sights Index

FEATURES

Sahara	*Eating*
Teatro La Fenice	*Entertainment*
Orange	*Drinking*
Caffè	*Café*
Banco Rosso	*Highlights*
Nave de Oro	*Shopping*
Brussa	*Sights/Activities*
Hotel Galleria	*Sleeping*

AREAS

	Beach, Desert
	Building
	Land
	Mall
	Other Area
	Park/Cemetary
	Sports
	Urban

HYDROGRAPHY

	River, Creek
	Intermittent River
	Canal
	Swamp
	Water

BOUNDARIES

	State, Provincial
	International
	Ancient Wall

ROUTES

	Tollway
	Freeway
	Primary Road
	Secondary Road
	Tertiary Road
	Lane
	Under Construction
	One-Way Street
	Unsealed Road
	Mall/Steps
	Tunnel
	Walking Path
	Walking Trail
	Track
	Walking Tour

TRANSPORT

	Airport, Airfield
	Bus Route
	Cycling, Bicycle Path
	Ferry
	General Transport
	Metro
	Monorail
	Rail
	Taxi Rank
	Tram

SYMBOLS

	Bank, ATM
	Buddhist
	Castle, Fortress
	Christian
	Diving, Snorkeling
	Embassy, Consulate
	Hospital, Clinic
	Information
	Internet Access
	Islamic
	Jewish
	Lookout
	Monument
	Mountain
	National Park
	Parking Area
	Petrol Station
	Picnic Area
	Point of Interest
	Police Station
	Post Office
	Ruin
	Swimming Pool
	Telephone
	Toilets
	Zoo, Bird Sanctuary
	Waterfall